GEORGE W. BUSH

President in a Turbulent World

Pam Zollman

E **Enslow Publishers, Inc.**
40 Industrial Road
Box 398
Berkeley Heights, NJ 07922
USA

http://www.enslow.com

To Mike and Colleen Wright
for everything that you do for me

Library of Congress Cataloging-in-Publication Data

Zollman, Pam.
    George W. Bush : President in a turbulent world / by Pam Zollman.
      p. cm. — (People to know today)
    Includes bibliographical references and index.
    ISBN 0-7660-2628-0
    1. Bush, George W. (George Walker), 1946– .—Juvenile literature. 2. Presidents—
United States—Biography—Juvenile literature. 3. United States—Politics and
government—2001—Juvenile literature. 4. Iraq War, 2003—Juvenile literature.
I. Title. II. Series.
    E903.Z65 2005
    973.931092–dc22

                                       2005034892

Printed in the United States of America

10 9 8 7 6 5 4 3 2 1

To Our Readers: We have done our best to make sure all Internet Addresses in this book were
active and appropriate when we went to press. However, the author and the publisher have no
control over and assume no liability for the material available on those Internet sites or on
other Web sites they may link to. Any comments or suggestions can be sent by e-mail to
comments@enslow.com or to the address on the back cover.

Every effort has been made to locate all copyright holders of material used in this book. If
any errors or omissions have occurred, corrections will be made in future editions of this
book.

Photo credit: AP/Wide World, pp. 1, 4, 8, 37, 49, 57, 59, 62, 65, 68, 70, 74, 76,
78, 79, 80, 81, 87, 91, 95, 98, 102, 108, 111; George Bush Presidential Library,
pp. 7, 12, 14, 16, 18, 22, 28, 35, 43, 46, 51.

Cover Illustration: AP/Wide World

CONTENTS

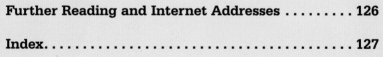

George Walker Bush

1
RUNNING
FOR OFFICE

George Walker Bush and his friends were sitting around the kitchen table at Joe O'Neill's home in the summer of 1977. Bush had graduated from business school at Harvard and moved back to Midland, Texas, his hometown. He was working in the oil business, but a political opportunity had arisen.

Representative George Mahon, a Democrat who had represented Midland in Congress for forty-three years, was retiring. In a surprise move, Bush announced his candidacy.

"Why do you want to do this?" asked Joe O'Neill.

Bush looked around the table. "Are you gonna do it? Are you gonna do it?" When no one spoke up, Bush said, "Well then, I am."[1]

At thirty-one, Bush had a skimpy résumé but a highly

recognizable family name. His father, George H.W. Bush, had been a congressman from Texas, an ambassador, head of the CIA, and was then seriously considering a presidential campaign.

What the younger Bush lacked in experience, he made up for in friends, family connections, and enthusiasm. His friends around that table became his campaign staff. His family helped him campaign. Family members and his father's friends donated generously.

Bush had worked in his father's campaigns and had helped with other Republican campaigns. He felt confident about his chances in the primary. "The opposition will not be of any concern to me," he told the *Lubbock* (Texas) *Avalanche-Journal.*[2]

Together, he and his wife, Laura, drove across the Texas Panhandle. Bush gave speeches, shook hands, and talked to anyone who would listen.

His opponents in the Republican primary took similar stands on issues. A primary is an election within a political party. Registered voters choose who they want to run for office, representing their party.

Candidate Jim Reese, the Odessa mayor, claimed that Bush was a liberal Yankee. Reese also attacked Bush's father and Bush's position on the Trilateral Commission, a controversial group of international political and business leaders.[3] Texans tended to be suspicious of anything that sounded like a one-world government.

George W. Bush was not a member of the Trilateral

George W. and Laura Bush traveled across Texas to win votes.

Commission, but rumors about it would not go away. This frustrated his campaign.

Many saw Bush's congressional campaign as a preview of the Republican primary for the presidency. His father, George H.W. Bush, was planning to run against Ronald Reagan to become the Republican candidate. When Reagan backed George W. Bush's opponent, Jim Reese, and donated money to Reese's campaign, it seemed especially true. Why else would Reagan be interested in Texas Panhandle politics?

However, George W. Bush proved to be a formidable competitor. He forced Reese into a runoff, and then won the runoff. A runoff is an extra election between the two top candidates. Bush's victory brought out a cockiness that was not appreciated. "Bush was acting like a

Would Bush be elected to Congress?

little kid. He was an immature rich-kid brat," said Mel Turner, a fellow Republican and well-known radio personality in the area.[4]

Some of Turner's negative feelings stemmed from a luncheon meeting where Turner had bluntly asked George W. Bush if anyone in the Bush family was involved in the Trilateral Commission. Bush refused to answer or to shake Turner's hand as he left the luncheon. Bush also cursed Turner as he walked out.[5]

George W. Bush's Democratic opponent was State Senator Kent Hance, who had grown up in Lubbock, Texas. Hance emphasized Bush's Ivy League college background and pointed out that most of George W. Bush's campaign contributions were from "outsiders," big names who did not live in Texas.

In his first television ad, Bush was shown jogging. Hance commented that no one jogs in Muleshoe, Texas, unless he is running from something.[6] Bush's campaign began unraveling after that. He was trying to run a "nice-guy" campaign, and was caught off guard by his opponents' tactics. "It was my first confrontation with cheap-shot politics," Bush said.[7]

Just days before the election, Hance revealed that a Texas Tech student had run an ad in the college's newspaper for a Bush campaign rally some months before. The student, a Bush campaign volunteer, promised free beer at the rally. Bush had had no prior knowledge about the promise. Hance mailed a letter to all Church of Christ members.

This "Dear Fellow Christian" letter stated that Bush was using free beer to buy votes from the college kids. Hance had known about the incident for several months, but he waited until the last minute so Bush would have little time to react to the charges.

Bush did not respond, even though he had discovered that Hance owned a local bar where Texas Tech students gathered. Bush could have used this information against Hance but decided against it. "I'm not going to ruin the guy in his home town. He's not a bad person," Bush told his staffers.[8]

Bush and his wife, Laura, watched the televised election returns with friends. Lubbock, Kent Hance's hometown, went to Hance. Bush knew then he had lost the election. The final count was 53,917 for Hance and 47,497 for Bush. "I finished a popular second," said Bush.[9]

Bush called to congratulate Hance on the win. Hance said, "I never detected any bitterness."[10] Because of that, a friendship grew between the two men. The friendship became even stronger after Hance became a Republican in 1985.

"Frankly, getting whipped was probably a pretty good thing for me," Bush said.[11] Although George W. Bush would wait a long time before he tried again, this was the first and last political race he would lose.

2
GROWING UP IN MIDLAND, TEXAS

George Walker Bush was born on July 6, 1946, in New Haven, Connecticut. His father, George Herbert Walker Bush, known to his family as Poppy, was a student at Yale University. Poppy had enrolled after serving in the navy during World War II. George W.'s mother, Barbara Pierce Bush, worked in the campus bookstore for a short time.

His parents called their firstborn "Little George" or "Georgie," because he shared his father's first name. As he got older, friends and family called him "George W." Their full names are not exactly the same, so George W. is not a "Junior."

In 1948 Poppy graduated from Yale. He accepted a job with Dresser Industries, which had several oil-related businesses, and moved his family to Odessa, Texas. They moved

Baby George had a big grin for his parents in this 1947 photo.

to California the next year so that Poppy could train at another Dresser company. George W.'s sister Robin was born there in 1949.

The Bush family moved back to Texas in 1950 and settled in Midland. Poppy started his own oil company with a neighbor. The third Bush child, John Ellis, called "Jeb," was born in 1953. That turned out to be a painful year for the Bush family.

One spring morning in 1953, Robin was too tired to go outside and play. George W.'s mother thought something was wrong with the three-year-old. Tests revealed that Robin had leukemia. At that time there was no cure.

George W. was never told that Robin would die. "We felt it would have been too big a burden for such a little fellow," his mother, Barbara, explained.[1] Robin was taken to a hospital in New York City for treatment. Six-year-old George W. and baby Jeb stayed with friends in Midland for the next few months.

George W. was just seven years old when Robin died in November 1953. His parents drove to his school to tell him. He and a friend were carrying a record player from their classroom to the principal's office. "I remember seeing them pull up and thinking I saw my little sister in the back of the car," said George W.[2] He put the record player down and ran to the car. But, of course, Robin was not there. His parents told him the bad news.

"I was sad, and stunned," said George W. "I knew Robin had been sick, but death was hard for me to imagine."[3] He spent the next few weeks trying to cheer up his grief-stricken parents. George W. told jokes and clowned around to make his mother smile. One day she overheard George W. telling a friend that he could not

Leukemia

Leukemia is cancer of blood cells. Cancer is a disease that causes abnormal cells to grow and not function properly. The cause of leukemia is unknown. There are two main types: (1) acute leukemia has blood cells that cannot function at all and the patient quickly becomes worse; (2) chronic leukemia has blood cells that function somewhat and it takes much longer for the patient to grow worse. Acute leukemia is most common in children. Today, doctors can cure many patients with acute leukemia. There is still no cure for chronic leukemia.[4]

come out to play because he could not leave his mother. She needed him.

Barbara Bush said, "That started my cure. I realized I was too much of a burden for a little seven-year-old boy to carry."[5] George W. and his mother formed a very strong bond. The memory of Robin never faded, but the painful grief eventually did.

George W. attended Sam Houston Elementary School, walking there with his friends. Sometimes his dog Nicky would follow him to school. George W. was on the safety patrol at school and played Little League baseball.

George always loved baseball.

The Bush family was growing. Neil was born in 1955, and Marvin was born in 1956. Three years later, Dorothy, nicknamed "Doro," was born.

Poppy moved the family to Houston in 1959 so he would be closer to his company's oil rigs in the Gulf of Mexico. George W. went to Kinkaid, a private school, for two years.

The year before, in Midland, he had been on the football team and elected class president. At Kinkaid, he made friends easily.

Once again George W. played on the football team and was elected to a class office.

Two years later, in 1961, his parents decided to send George W. to a boarding school. George H.W. Bush had gone to Phillips Academy in Andover, Massachusetts. Andover, as it is called, is an exclusive prep school. "I was fifteen and on my own for the first time in my life," said George W.[6]

At Andover George W. met Clay Johnson, another Texan, and they became lifelong friends. Together they learned to cope at the all-boys boarding school. They had to wear coats and ties to class and attend chapel five days a week.

George W. did not do well on his first English paper. The assignment was to write about emotion, so he decided to write about his sister Robin. Wanting to impress his new teacher, he looked up another word for "tears" in his thesaurus. He chose "lacerates," not realizing that it was a verb (to rip) instead of a noun. The only impression made was the zero on his paper. It was marked so hard that "it stuck out of the back side of the blue book," said George W.[7]

"And my math grades weren't all that good either to begin with. So I was struggling," he added.[8]

Once again, George W. made friends easily. He played sports, then joined the cheerleading squad and was head cheerleader in his senior year. He formed a rock-and-roll band called the Torqueys, though he did

The Bush family in 1956: Ten-year-old George W., with his parents and three younger brothers, Jeb (standing), Neil, and baby Marvin.

not play an instrument. He also did not sing. Instead, he clapped his hands in time to the music.

George W. gave himself the title of "High Commissioner of Stickball," and turned the game into a fun sport to play after dinner. Students did not have to be coordinated or talented to be on a team. George W. organized the teams into a league and had a tournament that drew cheering fans.

"How we missed him," said his mother. Every day she looked for a letter from George W. When it finally came, Barbara hurriedly opened it. "It started out, 'Last weekend was the greatest in my life. . . .' I burst into tears. Our boy had 'the best weekend of his life' without us! How silly that seems now and just a tad selfish."[9]

"I missed my parents and brothers and sister. It was a shock to my system. But I buckled down, worked hard, and learned a lot," George W. said.[10]

He studied hard, but was always just an average student. Tom Lyons, the history teacher at Andover, awakened George W.'s love for the subject. This love of history has stayed with George W. throughout his life. He chose history as his major in college. "Andover taught me how to think . . . in a way I never had before," said George W. "Andover taught me the power of high standards. . . . Andover taught me independence."[11]

George W., right, with his family after church in Houston in 1964.

3

COLLEGE AND THE NATIONAL GUARD

Georg e W. Bush wanted to go to Yale University, the school his father and grandfather had attended. He applied, but was afraid his mediocre academic record at Andover would keep him out. He also applied to the University of Texas, where he hoped his chances might be better. "My recollection," said Bush's friend Doug Hannah, "was that he was shocked when he got into Yale."[1]

Colleges often use factors other than grades to judge students, such as athletic ability and minority status. Giving an edge to the children of alumni, called a legacy policy, is common practice. The colleges hope to build family loyalties that will lead to larger donations to the school.

That summer of 1964, Bush went home to Houston. His father was running for the U.S. Senate, so George W.

helped with the campaign. He compiled a book for all 254 Texas counties, with the names and phone numbers of local leaders. These books also summarized the main industries and businesses in each county.

He also passed out campaign literature and signs, organized rallies, and clapped the loudest at his father's speeches. At eighteen, George W. was quickly learning about politics.

In the fall, he started his freshman year at Yale. His roommates were two friends from Andover, Rob Dieter and Clay Johnson. They roomed together for all four years at Yale. Once again, as he had done at Andover, George W. made a point to know everyone.

"George was the person who in three months knew the name of everybody and actually knew fifty percent of the class," Roland W. Betts said.[2]

Betts is a close friend of Bush's from Yale. He said

> **At eighteen, George W. was quickly learning about politics.**

Bush would walk up to strangers on campus and introduce himself. "That's just his nature," Betts explained. "He's not pretentious, not exploitive. George is a very disarmingly, charming person."[3]

For George H.W. Bush, the Senate race in Texas ended in defeat. George W. had flown home to Houston to be with his father on election night. When the results came in and Democrat Ralph Yarborough won, George W. cried.[4]

When he returned to the Yale campus, Bush went to see the Reverend William Sloan Coffin Jr., the Yale chaplain. Reverend Coffin had been a friend of his father's when they had both attended Yale. Instead of getting sympathy for his father's defeat, Bush was stunned by the chaplain's response. "Frankly, he was beaten by a better man," Coffin told Bush.[5] This comment hurt Bush, because he is fiercely loyal to his father. A disheartened George W. ignored politics for a brief time. He showed no interest in national events or in joining campus political clubs.

However, he was interested in pledging at a fraternity. In his sophomore year, Bush joined Delta Kappa Epsilon, or Deke, as it is often called. Deke attracted campus athletes and sports fans. Bush loved sports and fit in well. The Dekes elected him president of the fraternity in 1967, his junior year. The Dekes were known for their wild parties. Bush drank a lot with his fraternity brothers, and this got him into trouble.

One Christmas, Bush and his buddies decided to steal a wreath for the Deke House. They were very drunk and noisy, so the police stopped them to ask what was going on. Bush told them, and the police arrested him and his friends. "We were apprehended for disorderly

> **"He's not pretentious, not exploitive. George is a very disarmingly, charming person."**

Bush did more socializing than studying at Yale.

conduct; we apologized and the charges were dropped," Bush later explained.[6]

Another run-in with the police occurred at a football game against Princeton. Yale won and everyone was so excited that they tried to tear down Princeton's wooden goalposts. Bush was sitting on top of the goalpost when Princeton's campus police arrived on the scene. The police took everyone, including Bush, to the campus station. They were ordered to leave town.[7]

During summer breaks, Bush returned to Houston. The summer after his freshman year, in 1965, he worked on an oil rig, a job arranged for him by his father. The company, Circle Drilling, was located in Lake Charles, Louisiana, not far from Houston.

The crew would work a week on the oil rig, located offshore in about twenty feet of water. Then they would have a week off, and Bush would head back to Houston to be with his friends. He was supposed to work from June through August. Instead, he quit one week ahead of schedule, and his father called him into his office. "I just want you to know that you have disappointed me," his father said.[8]

"Those were the sternest words to me," George W. said, "even though he said them in a very calm way. When you love a person and he loves you, those are the harshest words someone can utter. I left that office realizing I had made a mistake."[9]

In 1966, Bush's summer jobs were working at Sears and helping his father with another political campaign. George H.W. Bush was running for Congress, and this time he was elected. George W. was also growing closer to Cathryn Wolfman, a young woman he had begun dating when he was home for Christmas in Houston. She was a student at Rice University.

During the summer of 1967, Bush worked for a month as a bookkeeper. He spent the rest of the summer with Cathryn Wolfman, who was by this time his fiancée. The engagement had been announced in the *Houston Chronicle* on New Year's Day 1967, though no date was set for the wedding.

With Bush at Yale and Wolfman at Rice, the couple had found that maintaining a long-distance relationship was difficult. They remained engaged through the summer of 1967 and into the fall, when they headed back to school, but they eventually changed their plans. "We grew apart because we spent so much time apart," Cathy Wolfman explained.[10]

The Vietnam War

In 1954, after a long conflict, Vietnam, which had been a French colony, was divided into two warring parts: North Vietnam had a Communist government, and South Vietnam was an ally of the United States. Under Communism, the government controls the economy and outlaws free enterprise. In 1962, the United States sent troops to help South Vietnam defend itself against Communism. As more U.S. troops were sent to Vietnam in the next few years, many Americans protested U.S. involvement. Peace negotiations began in 1968, mainly in response to the antiwar movement in the United States. U.S. troops were gradually withdrawn starting in 1969. A cease-fire was declared in January 1973. Millions had died in the conflict, including some 58,000 U.S. troops. Vietnam was united as a Communist country in 1976.[11]

As a senior at Yale, Bush was invited to join Skull and Bones, a secret society on campus. Only fifteen students are asked to join each year. The society is so secret that its members are forbidden to talk about it. Bush's father and grandfather had both been members of Skull and Bones.

As graduation loomed in the spring of 1968, Bush had to decide what to do next. He was graduating with a C average and a degree in history. He could not make any career plans until he knew what would happen with his military status. The United States was at war, struggling to win against Communism in Vietnam. In January 1968, the fighting got worse, and more troops were needed in February.

Today the United States has an all-volunteer military. But during the Vietnam War, men were drafted into the service for two years, unless they were still in school. All young men had to register for the draft when they turned eighteen.

Many people protested

against the war in Vietnam. They did not think the United States could win the war or should even be involved. Casualties were high, and there appeared to be no end to the war. Some men burned their draft cards or fled to Canada to avoid the draft. "I knew I would serve. Leaving the country to avoid the draft was not an option for me; I was too conservative and too traditional," Bush said.[12]

George H.W. Bush had been a navy fighter pilot in World War II. He had been shot down over the Pacific Ocean and had received the Distinguished Flying Cross.

George W. decided that he wanted to be a pilot, too. If he waited to be drafted, he would be assigned to the infantry, where he would be a soldier fighting on the ground.

> **"I knew I would serve. Leaving the country to avoid the draft was not an option for me; I was too conservative and too traditional."**

Bush decided to try the National Guard. His chances of going to Vietnam would be considerably lower. The National Guard maintains units that are ready to deal with national emergencies or mobilize for war. It is a partner with the U.S. military.

There were few National Guard openings and long waiting lists. Even though some people may not agree with the practice, it was common for exceptions to be made for sons of prominent people. The sons of Congressman George H.W. Bush and Senator Lloyd Bentsen both ended up in the same Texas National Guard unit.

Since the Texas National Guard was an agency of the state, applicants could be recommended by the governor, lieutenant governor, or Speaker of the House. Ben Barnes, then Speaker of the House and a Democrat, later said that although he helped many influential families' sons get in the National Guard, he did not remember if he helped George W., whose family was strongly Republican. "Nobody could ever [recall], and my staff was divided if I did or did not," Barnes said.[13]

During his Christmas 1967 vacation, Bush told Lieutenant Colonel Walter "Buck" Staudt that he wanted to be a pilot like his father. Lieutenant Colonel Staudt was commander of the 147th Fighter Group of the Texas Air National Guard.

Bush wanted to be a pilot like his father.

There were openings for pilots, which required almost two years of flight training, plus four years of part-time service. The personnel officer for the 147th Fighter Group was Colonel Rufus G. Martin. "It was very difficult to find someone who would commit himself to the rigorous training that was required," he said.[14] At the time George W. Bush applied, there were four slots for pilots available. The selection would be made based on the applicant's age, college degree, and performance on written and oral tests.

One slot was given to Bush. Staudt wrote on Bush's paperwork, "Applicant is a quiet, intelligent young man who has the interest, motivation and knowledge necessary to become a commissioned officer."[15]

After basic training at Lackland Air Force Base in San Antonio, Texas, Bush was sent to Moody Air Force Base in Georgia, where he spent the next year in flight school. Returning to Houston in December 1969, he trained on F-102s and impressed his superiors with his abilities.

During the Cold War years, the stated mission of the Texas Air National Guard was to defend the Gulf Coast and South Texas against bombers, especially those from the Soviet Union.[16] There had been a program called Palace Alert that used F-102s in Vietnam. They were armed with Falcon missiles and would fly beside B-52s during air patrols. There were not enough F-102 pilots during the Vietnam War because the plane was considered obsolete. The Palace Alert program was canceled.

Bush trained on F-102s and impressed his superiors with his abilities.

On June 23, 1970, after two years of active duty, Bush graduated from Combat Crew Training School. He still flew the F-102s several times a month as his

Bush learned to fly fighter
jets in the Texas Air National
Guard.

part-time duty, but he did not have a job
or any prospects for one.

Bush also did not have a steady girlfriend, even
though he dated frequently. He lived at an apartment
complex in Houston that was known for its parties. His
future wife, Laura Welch, lived there as well, but they did
not meet until much later. "I was rootless," Bush says of
that time in his life.[17]

He worked for a few months for an agribusiness
company, where he did well. But he found the job
boring, so he quit. Bush called it "a stupid coat-and-tie

job."[18] Office work was too dull in comparison to his National Guard duties.

Winton M. "Red" Blount asked Bush to be the political director in his campaign for the Senate. Blount was running against a longtime Democratic incumbent in Alabama. An incumbent is the person who already holds an office. In May 1972 the National Guard transferred Bush's weekend duties to the 187th Tactical Reconnaissance Group in Montgomery, Alabama. So Bush moved to Alabama and worked there until the November election, which Blount lost.

Bush's parents had moved to Washington, D.C. His father was considering becoming chairman of the Republican National Committee.

George W. still had some growing up to do. When he visited his family at Christmastime in 1972, he got into trouble because of alcohol. He and Marvin, his fifteen-year-old brother, had gone out together. George W. had been drinking heavily and hit a neighbor's trashcan as he drove down his parents' street. His father, of course, was displeased. Not interested in a lecture, George W. challenged his father. "You want to go mano a mano right here?" he demanded.[19]

Doro Bush said, "My dad did not think that was attractive or funny or nice."[20] George H.W. Bush helped his son get a counseling job with Professionals United for Leadership (PULL). It was a mentoring program for poor African-American boys. John L. White, a former tight end for the Houston Oilers football team and the elder Bush's friend, had organized the program. George H.W. Bush hoped that this job would help give his son some purpose in life.

George W. often took Marvin with him to the warehouse on McGowen Street where PULL was located. "He was a super, super guy," said "Big Cat" Ernie Ladd, a professional football player who was also a mentor at PULL.[21]

Muriel Simmons Henderson, one of the senior counselors for PULL, said, "He was so down to earth. . . . You could not help liking him. He was always fun."[22]

Finally Bush decided to get serious about a career, so he applied to the University of Texas law school. He was rejected, so he applied to Harvard Business School. He did not tell his family. One of Bush's Yale classmates, Clayton Day Jr., said, "He went there for the same reason a lot of us did. I had a lot of degrees, but I couldn't do anything. It was like trade school."[23]

> **Finally Bush decided to get serious about a career.**

Bush needed only eight more months to fulfill his six-year commitment with the National Guard. The Guard transferred him to a Boston unit, so he could attend Harvard Business School. They then gave him an early release, which many say was not uncommon at the time.

Bush's National Guard record would become a hotly

debated issue many years later when he pursued a career in political office. Critics would say that in Boston, Bush stopped reporting for duty, lost his flight status, and failed to take a physical. Supporters would counter that it is common practice for the National Guard to allow men to transfer to another unit either permanently or temporarily as a way of keeping them on the active list—even when the units do not need the transferees. As for the physical: With limited hours, they say, it is not uncommon to miss the deadline.

At Harvard, Bush did not fit the image of a typical business school student. He dressed in scruffy clothes, chewed tobacco, and did not know where he was going after graduation. At twenty-seven, he was older than the other students, and this time his studies came easier. "I went there to actually learn," Bush says. "And I did."[24]

"Harvard gave me the tools and the vocabulary of the business world," he said. "It taught me the principles of capital, how it is accumulated, risked, spent, and managed."[25] In 1975, Bush earned his master of business administration (MBA) degree from Harvard. It was now time to put these newly acquired skills to work.

> At **Harvard**, Bush **did not fit** the **image** of a **typical** business school **student.**

4

THE OIL BUSINESS— BOOM TO BUST

After his Harvard graduation, Bush visited his parents in China. His father was the chief of the U.S. Liaison Office in the People's Republic of China. There, George W. saw a society without free enterprise. "Every bicycle looked the same. People's clothes were all the same—drab and indistinguishable," Bush said later.[1]

This experience made him want to start his own business. As soon as he returned to the United States, he packed his car and drove to Midland, Texas, where he had grown up. His father had been successful in the oil industry, and George W. wanted to try his luck there, too. He had spent one summer on an oil rig, so he knew some of the essentials of the trade. His business degree from Harvard had prepared him for running a business.

In the 1970s, Midland was "entrepreneurial heaven,"

Bush said of his hometown.[2] Oil prices were high and there was lots of action in the energy business. It was still a boom time, and people could get rich, as his father had done two decades earlier.

After Bush rented an apartment, family friends from Midland took him under their wing. The research skills he had honed studying history at Yale came in handy. He started as a freelance "land man," learning the oil business from the ground up.

A land man researches the land records in a courthouse to learn what mineral and oil rights are available for lease. Bush obtained this information for oil companies

His father had been successful in the oil industry, and George W. wanted to try his luck there, too.

and then sometimes negotiated the deals as well. "Geologists decide where to buy the leases. Land men deal with people. George was ideal for that," said Paul Rea, geologist and president of the oil-drilling company Spectrum 7.[3]

A land man can also invest in drilling wells. With his knowledge of mineral rights, Bush had an advantage. He invested the money left over from his education bank account. Although he did not make a lot of money in these investments, he also did not lose a lot either.

After a year as a land man, Bush started Arbusto Energy, his own oil exploration company. Arbusto, pronounced "Ar-*boos*-toe," means "bush" in Spanish. His uncle Jonathan Bush persuaded family friends to invest in the company. After Arbusto hit a number of dry wells, people started pronouncing the company name "Ar-*BUST*-o."

Bush was a bachelor, and he lived like one. His apartment looked as if a Texas tornado had plowed through it. Dirty clothes and newspapers were everywhere. His bed had broken, so he fixed it with several

neckties knotted together. He dated, but did not have a serious girlfriend. And he partied. His friends called him "Bombastic Bushkin" and teased him about bringing his East Coast college lifestyle back to Midland.

Bush was a bachelor, and he lived like one.

Once again Bush's drinking got him into trouble. In 1976 he was visiting his parents in Maine over Labor Day weekend. George W. took his seventeen-year-old sister, Doro; tennis star John Newcombe; and Newcombe's wife to a local bar.

After having too many beers, George W. attempted to drive back to the Bush family home in Kennebunkport. His erratic driving caused the police to pull him over. Bush failed the sobriety test and was charged with drunk driving. He paid the hefty fine and his driver's license was briefly suspended.

When a Texas congressional seat opened up in the summer of 1977, Bush announced that he was going to run for Congress. A couple of weeks later, his friends Joe and Jan O'Neill invited him to a barbecue. They wanted him to meet Jan's close friend Laura Welch.

Laura was a librarian at an elementary school in Austin, Texas. She often visited her parents in Midland, where she had grown up. Mutual friends had been saying nice things to Laura about George W. Laura finally agreed to meet him.

As children, George W. and Laura had lived half a mile from each other and had attended the same junior high, but they had never met. They had also lived at the

George and Laura crossed paths many times before they actually met through friends.

same apartment complex in Houston, but had never crossed paths.

The O'Neills' barbecue was in August. Always the first to arrive at a party and the first to leave, George W. normally left around 9 P.M. This time, however, he stayed until midnight. The O'Neills knew he was smitten with Laura Welsh.

Laura and George W. spent the next day playing miniature golf. The following weekend, he visited Laura in Austin. He had cut short a visit with his parents in Maine because he wanted to go home to see Laura. "If it wasn't love at first sight, it happened shortly thereafter," George W. said.[4]

Their friends were surprised that the matchmaking actually worked. The couple seemed to be opposites. Laura was quiet; George W. was loud. Laura preferred reading a book; George W. loved parties and crowds. "She is totally at ease, comfortable and natural, just calm," George W. has said of Laura. "I, on the other hand, am perpetual motion."[5]

> "If it wasn't **love** at **first sight**, it **happened** shortly **thereafter.**"

After a whirlwind courtship, George W. proposed to Laura, later calling it "the best decision I have ever made."[6] Bush's parents were just as surprised as his friends. Barbara Bush said, "The day after we got home from our China trip, George W. came to Houston with

George W. and Laura Bush posed for a wedding day portrait with the groom's parents, Barbara and George H.W. Bush.

a beautiful young woman and announced they were getting married."[7]

Three months after they met, George W. Bush and Laura Welch were married on November 5, 1977. Neither of them wanted a big wedding. They limited the invitations to seventy-five guests and kept the ceremony simple.

Their honeymoon in Mexico was brief, because Bush had to hit the campaign trail in his bid for a seat in Congress. Although he lost the race, he had gained a wife. She had a calming, organizing effect on his life. Even so, it did not stop his drinking.

> **Laura had a calming, organizing effect on his life. Even so, it did not stop his drinking.**

Meanwhile, George W.'s father was having better success in the political arena. In 1980, Ronald Reagan was elected president of the United States, and George H.W. Bush was his vice president.

Oil prices had risen in 1973 with the Arab oil embargo. When Iraq invaded Iran in 1979, oil production almost halted. Prices rose again. Crude oil prices rapidly increased from 1973 to 1981.

People wanted to invest their money. Banks made big loans, and people borrowed more than they could afford. Arbusto Energy was doing well. George W. pleased his investors by treating them honestly and

THE OIL BUSINESS—BOOM TO BUST

returning cash through each of his partnerships within Arbusto.

By 1981, Arbusto Energy had become Bush Exploration Company. The company went public in 1982, which meant it could now trade stock. This turned out to be a bad move, because the Texas oil industry had started to collapse.

OPEC is the Organization of the Petroleum Exporting Countries. A few OPEC member nations started oversupplying crude oil to the world. This caused oil prices to go down. "My little company was not very well prepared for the public markets and the program was not successful," Bush says. He tried a different approach by selling company stock to an investor.[8]

Another oil-drilling company, Spectrum 7, provided a good opportunity. Bush Exploration and Spectrum 7 merged in 1984, and George W. Bush became the chairman.

The price of oil had peaked in 1980 at almost $40 a barrel. After that, oil prices fell fast, down to $29 a barrel in late 1983.[9] Many companies and related industries were suffering or going out of business. People were losing their businesses, and sometimes their homes as well. Midland residents began withdrawing money from the banks. A monetary crisis resulted.

The collapse of First National Bank of Midland in 1983 indicated the end of the oil boom. This bank had been part of the oil industry for most of the twentieth

The End of the Oil Boom

Of the ten largest banks in Texas, nine failed between 1980 and 1994. Almost six hundred small banks failed in Texas during this time period as well.[10] The FDIC investigated and concluded, "Oil was both the foundation of the region's economy and the primary force behind the region's banking crisis."[11] The Federal Deposit Insurance Corporation, or FDIC, is an independent agency that was created by Congress in 1933. The FDIC's role is to help keep the United States' banking system stable by supervising banks and insuring their deposits.[12]

century. Its failure triggered other banking failures across the southwestern United States.

This was the situation that Bush and others in the oil industry were in by 1985. Oil prices fell to $10 a barrel in April 1986. By mid-1986, crude oil prices had fallen below $10.[13] "The actual low point in Oklahoma was $8.25 in 1986, for good-quality sweet crude," said Wayne Swearingen, a Tulsa independent oil-man and consultant.[14]

Banks were failing, companies were failing, and Bush was worried that Spectrum 7 would be next because it was losing money. Even though Spectrum 7 was drilling oil, the company's assets of oil and gas were no longer worth as much as they had been even six months ago. They owed more than they could hope to pay back.

Bush's choices were to lay off his staff and wait for oil prices to rise again, find more investors, or find someone to buy out his company. There were no willing investors because of the banking situation, and Bush did not want his staff to be unemployed. So he searched for a large company to buy Spectrum 7.

"I'm all name and no money," said Bush.[15] It turned out that all George W. needed was his name. Harken Oil and Gas wanted to buy a distressed company and thought the Bush name might be a bonus. The buyout was completed in September 1986. Bush became a consultant, some of his employees stayed with Harken, and Bush's friends gave jobs to the rest of his staff.

For Bush, 1985 had been a hard year. He had to call up investors to tell them that he had dug another dry well and that they had lost their investment. It was a very humbling experience for him.

George H.W. Bush had been successful at Andover, at Yale, in the Air Force, in the oil business, and in politics. George W. could not duplicate his father's success. This was frustrating, and during his oil days, George W. started drinking even more.

In Midland, going to local bars and country clubs was one of the ways to meet people and make business contacts. "That's how . . . George got to know everybody in town," says Mark Owen, a geologist who worked for Bush. "He was great at raising money, putting deals together. That, in my mind was George's strength."[16]

Even though he was drinking more, Bush still got to work at 8 A.M. each day. He didn't leave until 5 P.M. or later. "I drank only after work, at night, never during the day," he says."[17]

His friends deny that Bush was an alcoholic, but said he could not stop. "Once he got started, he couldn't, didn't shut it off," his friend Don Evans explained.[18]

One of the symptoms of alcoholism is a lack of control over drinking and not being able to stop.[19] Although he may not have shown all of the signs of an alcoholic, he did have other symptoms, such as driving under the influence of alcohol and showing aggressive behavior while drinking.[20]

Bush's drinking was a problem at home. He and Laura had twin daughters, Barbara and Jenna, who had been born in November 1981. Laura did not want the girls to see their father drunk. Sometimes his loud voice would awaken them after he came home. Even though Laura and the twins were very important to George W., he still did not stop drinking.[21]

In the summer of 1985, the Reverend Billy Graham spent the weekend at the Bush family's Kennebunkport home. A well-known Southern Baptist minister, the Reverend Graham has traveled around the world, and his crusades attracted huge crowds of people who came to hear him speak.

Reverend Graham's visit made an impression on Bush. "He sat by the fire and talked. And what he said sparked a change in my heart," said Bush. "Reverend Graham planted a mustard seed in my soul, a seed that

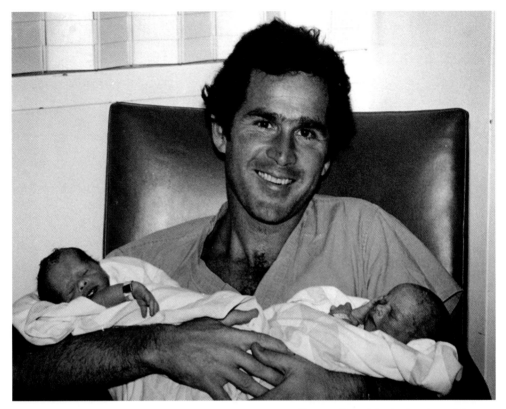

Even after his twin daughters Barbara and Jenna, were born, Bush was not ready to change his life.

grew over the next year. He led me to the path and I began walking."[22]

Bush had never before let religion guide his life. As a child, he had attended both Presbyterian and Episcopalian churches and had been an altar boy. Later, he taught Sunday school. He joined Laura's church, the First Methodist Church of Midland, after they married. But it was not until he spent the weekend with the Reverend Graham that he began to take the Bible more seriously.

Bush began reading the Bible after he returned to Midland. That fall he and his friend Don Evans attended a weekly men's Bible study group. Bush studied several hours to prepare for each meeting.

However, Bush was still drinking too much alcohol, and it was putting a strain on his marriage. "When you're drinking," Bush said, "it can be an incredibly selfish act."[23]

The turning point for George W. and Laura came in 1986, the year of their fortieth birthdays. They planned a get-together with several friends who were also turning forty. George W.'s younger brother, Neil, also joined them for a weekend celebration in Colorado Springs, Colorado. At dinner, everyone drank several bottles of wine. The next morning George W. awoke with a bad hangover.

Normally he ran three or four miles every day, but that morning he struggled to finish his run. Back at the hotel, he told Laura he was not going to drink any more. "I quit drinking in 1986 and haven't had a drop since then," he later said.[24]

Bush discovered that he did not need alcohol. He was more disciplined without it. Bush could still be the funny, fun-loving guy that people enjoyed. And as he grew spiritually, he also discovered that his life was changing for the better. "Faith changes lives," he said. "I know, because faith has changed mine."[25]

Bush's oil career had gone from boom to bust, but his personal life switched from bust to boom.

5
POLITICS AND BASEBALL

O nce the sale to Harken Oil and Gas was final in September 1986, the company name changed to Harken Energy. George W. Bush stayed on Harken's Board of Directors and acted as a consultant.

After eight years as vice president, George H.W. Bush was running for president of the United States. In April 1987, George W. moved his family to Washington, D.C., to help with his father's campaign.

Laura did not want to move. She had dedicated herself to raising the twins. She was active at their school, volunteering for the PTO and school library. However, she understood her husband's desire to move.[1]

"He had an opportunity most people never get," said Laura Bush, "to work with his parent as adult to adult. If ever there was competition with his father," Laura said, "they had time to work through [it]."[2]

George W. Bush, with his family and his mother, at a campaign rally when George H.W. Bush was running for vice president on the ticket with Ronald Reagan.

George W. Bush became the loyalty enforcer. He checked reporters and campaign staff alike. He said, "I wanted to make sure the political managers of Dad's campaign were there to help elect a great man as President, not to make themselves look good."[3]

Lee Atwater, the presidential campaign strategist, had ties to George H.W. Bush's rivals in the primaries. This worried George W., so he asked Atwater directly if he could be trusted. Atwater told George W. to join the team, and that way he could keep an eye on Atwater. The two wound up becoming good friends.

George W. became an ambassador for his father, as well as a sounding board for the staff. Mary Matalin, who worked in the campaign and later served as George W.'s assistant, said, "He [George W.] was a general morale booster."[4]

George W.'s relationship with the press was the

opposite. He tended to view them with suspicion and hostility, making it his mission to squelch false rumors about his father. When a *Newsweek* reporter portrayed his father as a "wimp," George W. was irate. He wondered how anyone could believe that. George H.W. Bush had been a fighter pilot in World War II, a Yale athlete, and had started from the ground up in the oil business. To this day, memory of that article still upsets him. "I was furious," George W. said. "My blood pressure still goes up."[5]

George W. discovered that he did not like Washington, D.C. To him, it was full of self-important people who stepped on others to get ahead. After a year and a half in Washington, D.C., he had learned a valuable lesson: disloyalty was the worst sin of all.[6]

During this campaign, the two Bush families became even closer. Laura and her mother-in-law shared an interest in literacy. Barbara Bush had decided that she would focus on literacy if she became first lady. George W. and his father played golf together. The twins spent weekends with their grandparents.

> **George W. viewed the press with suspicion and hosility.**

After the debate with Democratic opponent Michael Dukakis, Barbara Bush asked George W. how he liked it. "He is the son who pulls no punches and tells it like he thinks it is," Barbara wrote in her journal. George W. confessed that he did not watch the debate, because he was too nervous. Instead, he went to a movie with his brother Marvin, but kept sending Marvin out to call friends to see how the debate was going.[7]

When the election was over, George H.W. Bush had been elected the forty-first president of the United States. His son could have had his pick of political offices. Instead, George W. went home to Texas.

Bush was not sure what he wanted to do, but he knew he wanted to step out of his father's shadow. He had tried his father's world and had had only a little success. So, when the opportunity to own a baseball team arose, Bush was quick to take it. He had always loved baseball.

During his father's campaign, George W. had learned that the Texas Rangers baseball team was for sale. Eddie Chiles, the Rangers' owner, was ill and wanted to sell. The Texas Rangers baseball team was very special to Chiles, and he wanted to make sure it stayed in Texas. So did baseball commissioner Peter Ueberroth.

William DeWitt Jr., who had been George W. Bush's business partner, wanted to know if Bush would put together a group of investors. Bush called his friends and formed a group to purchase the baseball team. Some were from Texas, but most were from other states, and this was a problem. So Bush found another investor, Richard Rainwater from Dallas. Rainwater called his friend Edward "Rusty" Rose, who also wanted to be part of the investment.

Bush merged the two groups and worked out a partnership with the thirty-nine investors. It was named BR Rangers, for the two men who would be managing the team, George W. Bush and Rusty Rose. Bush became the managing general partner, while Rose became the chairman of the board. "I had pursued the purchase like a pit bull on the pant leg of opportunity," said Bush.[8]

For his share of the investment, Bush used his Harken Energy stock as collateral to get a $500,000 loan.

Bush became an owner of the Texas Rangers baseball team.

Then he added another $106,000 of his own money for a total investment of $606,000, or 1.8 percent ownership of the Rangers. It was the smallest share. For his work putting together the deal, Bush would also get a 10 percent bonus if the partnership were to sell the Rangers. Baseball commissioner Ueberroth approved the sale, and the deal was signed on April 21, 1989. Bush was finally in his element.

In the 1980s, the Texas Rangers were a mediocre team, but they were developing a fan base. Another plus was that they had future Hall of Fame pitcher Nolan Ryan. A major problem, though, was the Rangers' rundown stadium in Arlington, Texas. The old stadium was not large enough, and a new stadium would attract new fans.

For three years Bush worked to get a new stadium built. Arlington is located between Fort Worth and Dallas. Fans from both big cities could easily drive there. In 1991, Arlington voters approved a half-cent tax increase for part of the new stadium. The BR Rangers paid for the rest. The new stadium was an instant success, and attendance doubled.

Bush made the Rangers a family affair. He took his family to every home game. Instead of watching games from the air-conditioned owner's box, Bush sat near the dugout. He propped his boots on the rail and ate sunflower seeds and popcorn. Bush liked being visible to the fans and signed as many autographs as the players did.

For the Bushes, baseball was a family affair. George W. threw out the opening pitch at this game in Oriole Park at Camden Yards in Baltimore, Maryland. Joining him were his nephew George P. Bush and his father, President Bush.

Just as he had done at Andover and Yale, Bush learned the names of everyone who worked for the Texas Rangers. His mother, Barbara Bush, was impressed. "George knew every living human, almost seemed like all 38,000! He introduced me to the 'best groundskeeper in the major leagues'; the 'finest ticket-taker in any park'; and the 'fastest hot dog vendor.' He knew them all!" his mother said after a visit.[9]

Bush's management abilities and the BR Rangers changed the Texas Rangers from a mediocre baseball team to one that made the playoffs in 1996. The team's gross revenue doubled in a few years, and the front-office staff went from 30 to 170.

Most people agree that the turning point in Bush's life was when he gave up drinking and became a born-again Christian. However, his Yale friend and BR Rangers partner Roland Betts disagreed, saying, "The turning point in his life was buying the Texas Rangers, succeeding with the Texas Rangers."[10]

> **Most people agree that the turning point in Bush's life was when he gave up drinking and became a born-again Christian.**

Two clouds on the horizon marred the blue skies of Bush's success, and both had to do with Harken Energy. In 1990, Bahraini officials approached Harken to drill offshore in their waters. Bahrain is a tiny island country in the Persian Gulf, east of Saudi Arabia. With a population approaching 678,000, Bahrain is three times the size of Washington, D.C. [11]

Bahrain was dependent on Saudi Arabia for oil. The country wanted to find more oil in its own waters, but large oil companies were not interested in drilling there. So officials from Bahrain contacted Harken Energy through a Houston oil consultant, Michael Ameen.

Some viewed this proposition as suspicious because Harken had no experience in offshore drilling. Critics claimed that Bahraini officials chose Harken because George W. Bush sat on the board, and it would be a good way to have a connection with the White House. However, Yousuf Shirawi, the Bahrain minister of development and industry, said that he was not "aware that George [W.] Bush was a member of the board."[12]

George W. himself warned against the deal. He pointed out that Harken did not have the experience and it would cost them too much. He also knew this deal would be viewed suspiciously by the press. And he was right. The media claimed it was a shady deal.

"The guy who didn't want into Bahrain was George W. Bush," said Michael Ameen, the Houston oil consultant who helped broker the deal. "He said, 'I don't think we have the expertise, we've never been overseas, and we don't have the money.'"[13] Bush turned out to be correct, and Harken never found oil.

That same year, a Los Angeles stockbroker, Ralph D.

Smith, had contacted members of the Harken board about selling some of their stock. Only Bush was interested. He could use the money to repay the $500,000 bank loan he had taken out for the Rangers deal.

He got approval to sell his stock from Harken's general counsel Larry E. Cummings. In June, Bush sold his stock for $835,307 before the end of a quarter.

In July Harken had operating losses in the second quarter and was being audited. Their losses for the second quarter of 1990 were three times higher than in 1989. Some people wondered if Bush had known about these losses before he sold the stock. That would have been illegal.[14] They also wondered if he knew ahead of time, through his father, that Iraq might invade Kuwait. Just six weeks after George W. sold his stock, the invasion of Kuwait occurred and the price of oil company stock—including Harken's—plummeted.

In 1991 the Securities and Exchange Commission (SEC) investigated the sale. The SEC regulates the market to protect investors. The SEC sent Bush a letter in 1993, telling him that they were suspending the inquiry: "The investigation has been terminated as to the conduct of Mr. Bush, and that at this time, no enforcement action is contemplated with respect to him."[15]

Overall, the Texas Rangers deal was a great personal success story for Bush. This spurred him to search for higher goals. Returning to politics, Bush set his sights on the governor's office.

6
THE GOVERNOR'S RACE

George W. Bush had wanted to run for governor of Texas in 1990, but he had a problem. He was still known as the president's son. His résumé was still pretty skimpy, and he knew that Texans would ask, "What's the boy ever done?"[1] So Bush had thrown himself into making the Texas Rangers baseball team successful and making himself visible. He signed baseball cards printed with his photo. He was on television almost every time a Rangers game was covered. And he worked hard to get the team an outstanding stadium.

Tom Schieffer, former president of the Rangers franchise, said that Bush brought more than a famous name to the Rangers: "He brought his ability to speak to people and tell them why it was fun to come to baseball games."[2]

Bush kept his eyes on the political front while

promoting baseball. "I like selling tickets," he said. "There are a lot of parallels between baseball and politics."[3]

On the Texas political scene, Democrat Ann Richards beat Republican Clayton Williams for governor in 1990. Ann Richards was a very popular governor. What Texans liked about her was her personality and sharp wit. Of course, not everyone agreed with her position on some issues.

One issue that provoked debate was her "Robin Hood" referendum. Richards had put forth a plan to change the way schools were funded in Texas. Property taxes went to the local school districts, which meant that schools in wealthy neighborhoods received more money. The plan Richards proposed would have put all the money in one pot to be passed out equally among all the school districts.

The "Robin Hood" referendum failed at the polls, with 63 percent of the voters rejecting it. A disappointed Ann Richards suggested that if Texans had better ideas, "those people should come forward and give us their plans."[4]

That seemed like the perfect invitation to George W. Bush, who decided to run against her in the 1994 election. He also decided that he would set the agenda of the election. He had observed that Bill Clinton had decided the issues in the 1992 presidential election, much to the

frustration of the elder Bush. "I wasn't going to let that happen to me," George W. said.[5]

Bush focused on only four issues

Bush announced his candidacy for governor of Texas at a rally in Houston, where one of his supporters was holding a sign that read, "NO MO' ANN!"

during the entire campaign. He believed in local control of schools, not state control. He worried about juvenile crime and the influence of gangs. He wanted to reform welfare in Texas and place time restrictions on benefits. And he wanted to eliminate frivolous lawsuits.

Bush did not use anyone on his staff who had been connected with his father's 1992 defeat. On that campaign, he had once again been the loyalty enforcer and morale booster. For his own political run, Bush sought out people whose first priority would be loyalty to him, not advancing their own careers.

The person he chose to lead his campaign was Karl Rove. They had first met when Rove worked as an assistant to Bush's father in 1973. Rove moved to Texas in 1977 to help George H.W. Bush run for Congress. Rove became George W.'s campaign strategist. Then George W. talked to Joe Allbaugh, who had helped Henry Bellmon win the 1986 governor's race in Oklahoma. Allbaugh agreed to manage George W.'s campaign. Bush was looking for a decisive personality, and he found it in Allbaugh.

Next, Bush asked Karen Hughes to join his campaign. She was a former television reporter who enjoyed covering politics. Hughes had worked for the Reagan-Bush campaign in 1984 as the Texas press coordinator. She became the campaign's communications director for George W. "Karen is someone who knows that it's so important to be proactive as opposed to defensive," Bush said.[6]

Now he was ready to take on Governor Ann Richards. The governor, well known for her wit, referred to her opponent as "Junior" or "Shrub" instead of Bush. But George W. Bush proved to be a strong campaigner. He traveled to all 254 Texas counties, visiting small town after small town. And in each place, he focused on the four issues of his campaign.

Even a mistake did not hurt his campaign. At one

point he wanted to go hunting. The press came along to cover the event. His guide pointed out a bird and Bush shot it. The press took pictures. Later it was discovered that the bird Bush held in his hand was not a dove. It was a killdee, a protected songbird, and it was illegal to shoot them. Bush bemoaned the fact that the press had a photo of him, dressed in hunting attire, "holding a shotgun in one hand and the wrong bird in the other."[7]

His staffers worried about what to do. Bush decided that he should confess. He contacted a local justice of the peace and paid the $130 fine. Next he called every reporter who had participated in the

Oh, no! Bush shot the wrong bird.

hunting trip and told them what had happened. "Thank goodness it was not deer season; I might have shot a cow," he said.[8] Voter reaction seemed to be one of understanding, that Bush had made a mistake and had admitted it. Instead of hurting his campaign, as some people felt it would, the incident may have helped it.

Later, at the Dallas State Fair, his daughter Jenna won a stuffed bird. She handed it to her father and said, "Look, Dad, a killdee."[9]

In Florida, George W.'s brother Jeb was running for governor. Their father was no longer in the White House, and felt it was best to stay out of his sons' campaigns.[10] Everyone thought that Jeb Bush would win easily in Florida. It was George W. they were worried about. Barbara Bush had her doubts, and George W. enjoyed needling her. "Even my own mother doesn't think I can win," he said.[11]

On Election Day, George W. and Laura arrived at the polls early. When he went to vote, George W. realized that he had forgotten his wallet. The poll workers waved him on through, saying that they recognized him. Bush won the election overwhelmingly, 54 percent to 45 percent. His brother, however, lost the Florida election.

"The joy is in Texas," said former President George H.W. Bush, "but our hearts are in Florida."[12]

After moving into the Governor's Mansion in Austin, Texas, George W. Bush got down to business. First on his agenda was promoting reading. He had watched his mother tutor his brother Neil in reading. Neil struggled with dyslexia, a learning disability. Barbara Bush had made literacy her project as first lady. Laura Bush, a former school librarian, also influenced him.

Before taking office, George W. Bush had gone on a fact-finding mission. He met several times with Barnet Alexander "Sandy" Kress, a Democrat on the Dallas school board. Dallas had successfully tried an accountability program for schools. If reading test scores went up, the schools were rewarded with extra money. They were penalized, however, if the scores went down. The program seemed to work, as reading scores went up.

First on his agenda was promoting reading.

Bush took notes during his meetings with Kress, wanting to know as much as possible about the reading situation in the schools. Kress was impressed: "Most politicians have a sound-bite view; some advisers come in with a little plan, and they speak it. His approach was exactly what a citizen would want."[13]

Kress gave Bush six names to call. To start, Bush discussed the problem with Dr. G. Reid Lyon, a reading expert at the National Institutes of Health in Maryland. The schools had stopped teaching phonics in favor of the whole language approach in the 1970s. Reading scores plummeted ever since whole language was introduced, though experts disagree on the reasons for this. In Texas

Governor Bush visited schools to emphasize the importance of reading skills.

in 1995, the state tests showed that ninety thousand kids could not pass the reading tests.

Bush worked with Kress and his education aide Margaret Spellings, as well as others, to develop legislation to improve reading scores. School funding was tied to test scores, and many schools started including phonics. The reading test scores rose dramatically.

Another problem Bush faced in 1998 was what to do about death row inmate Karla Faye Tucker, whose execution date was fast approaching. Tucker would be the first woman to be executed in Texas since 1863. That, coupled with the brutality of her crime and her later embrace of Christianity, caused a nationwide media sensation.

Many people came to her defense, claiming she was a different person now and should not die. Christian conservatives rallied around her, as did a juror from her trial.

Tucker appealed to Governor Bush. "I am in no way attempting to minimize the brutality of my crime," she wrote. "It obviously was very, very horrible and I do take full responsibility for what happened." She confessed to being "guilty. Very guilty."[14] She asked Bush to change her punishment from death to a life sentence. If he did, she promised to continue to reach out to others "to make a positive difference in their lives."[15]

Bush considered her argument but concluded that he could not step in

Karla Faye Tucker

High on drugs, twenty-three-year-old Tucker, Daniel Garrett, and Jimmy Leibrant decided to steal Jerry Dean's motorcycle. Tucker disliked Dean, who beat his wife, Karla's best friend. Robbery became brutal murder when they found Dean in bed with another woman, Deborah Thornton. While Leibrant waited outside, Tucker and Garrett killed Dean and Thornton with a hammer and a pickax.[16]

All three were arrested immediately because they had bragged about the murders. Leibrant testified against the other two at their trials. Tucker and Garrett were given the death penalty. Karla Faye Tucker became a born-again Christian in prison.

just because Tucker's newfound faith had changed her in a positive way. He asked, "How should Texas respond when a Muslim or Jew—or a Christian man—made the same argument?"[17]

In Texas, unlike other states, the governor cannot grant a pardon that legally releases a person from his punishment for violating the law. The governor also cannot change a person's prison sentence. A citizens' Board of Pardons and Paroles makes these decisions. If the board decides to allow an execution, all a Texas governor can do is grant a one-time thirty-day delay.

A thirty-day reprieve would have allowed Governor Bush to recommend to the Board of Pardons and Paroles that Tucker's sentence be changed. Then it would have been up to the board to reconsider Tucker's fate.

It was a hard choice to make. When Bush reviewed petitions, he asked two questions: (1) Is there any question about the person's guilt, and (2) Did the person have a fair hearing with full legal counsel? Bush decided not to grant the thirty-day delay.[18] Tucker was executed by lethal injection on February 3, 1998.

The decision did not affect Bush's run for reelection that year. Texans were pleased with his leadership and returned him to office. Bush beat out his Democratic opponent, Gary Mauro, by a landslide in November 1998. His reelection made history. He was the first Texas governor to win consecutive four-year terms.

When he became governor, Bush had put his share

of the Texas Rangers into an account called a blind trust. The BR Rangers sold the baseball team in 1998, and Bush received 12 percent of the profits, 10 percent of that as a bonus for putting together the partnership.

George W. Bush was ready to move on to a bigger playing field—running for the office of president of the United States.

The Bushes in the inaugural parade for his second term as governor of Texas.

7

RUNNING FOR
THE BIG PRIZE

Even as he ran for reelection as Texas's governor, people wondered if Bush would run for president in 2000. Polls in 1998 had shown that he was a favorite to be the Republican nominee. "I did not run for governor to be President of the United States," he said.[1] However, he began to consider the possibility and asked his family what they thought.

Laura Bush was reluctant, but the twins were against the idea altogether. In the fall, Barbara was headed for Yale and Jenna would attend the University of Texas. They wanted a normal life, without Secret Service agents accompanying them on dates. When their parents promised to try to keep them out of the spotlight, the twins finally okayed their father's campaign.

The Bush family bought 1,583 acres in Crawford,

Texas, near Waco. The Prairie Chapel Ranch was to be a refuge for the Bushes, away from the pressures of politics. The locals now call it the Texas White House.

To keep his commitment as governor of Texas, Bush attended the legislative sessions and waited until they were over before he hit the campaign trail. The Texas Legislature meets only once every two years for 140 days.[2]

Bush had run for governor as a "compassionate conservative," and it had worked well in the Texas elections. When he decided to run for president, he again ran as a compassionate conservative. "My vision includes everybody," Bush said. "It's described as compassionate conservative, but I emphasize the compassion."[3]

Because he was the favored front-runner in the presidential campaign and because he was the son of a former president, George W. Bush was more thoroughly examined by the press.

They focused on his C-average grades, criticizing his intellect, even though Vice President Al Gore, the Democratic nominee, earned only slightly better grades at Harvard. Also ignored was the fact that Bush's grades were better than Republican rival Senator John McCain's at the U.S. Naval Academy. Journalists disregarded his above-average SAT scores. Instead, the media concentrated on his tangled tongue when he spoke, mixing up words and phrases.[4]

For example, Bush had trouble pronouncing the

To explain the phrase "compassionate conservative," Bush has said that it is compassionate to help the needy, and conservative to require accountability and results.

word "nuclear" correctly. When he tried to say "tactical nuclear weapons," it came out "tacular nucular weapons." While discussing education policy, he said that the question to ask was, "Is our children learning?" And during a visit to a New Hampshire school, he told the students that a presidential candidate learns that "You've got to preserve." He meant persevere.[5]

Bush chose to ignore it all. He reminded the press that this had happened to him before in the 1994 campaign for Texas governor. "People said he's Daddy's boy," Bush told the reporters, "and they said he's not smart enough to be governor, he hasn't had the experience. Look who's standing here as governor of Texas."[6]

Bush disdained debates. He thought debates only displayed how eloquently a politician could speak. He said a debate felt like a charade.[7]

While Southern Methodist University was honoring Laura Bush, George W. missed the first of the three Republican primary debates, saying that he preferred to attend the SMU function and support his wife.[8]

A Boston television reporter gave Bush a pop quiz: Who was the new Pakistani leader after the military coup? Bush did not know. The press played and replayed this mistake. The impression remained that he had never left this country, much less knew anything about foreign affairs. Forgotten was the fact that Bush had spent time in China, Mexico, England, Scotland, Argentina, Gambia, and the Middle East.[9]

Condoleezza Rice came to the rescue. She was a high-ranking administrator at Stanford University. She had also been on President George H.W. Bush's national security team, keeping the former president current on foreign affairs.

Rice tutored George W. at his Crawford, Texas, ranch. They took long walks, going into steep canyons and across streams. One of the trails earned a new nickname, "Balkan Hill," because that is where Rice explained the Balkans situation to Bush.[10] There had been centuries of violence in the Balkans, a mountainous region in southeastern Europe. During the last decade, the Yugoslavian military killed thousands of Albanians

Condoleezza Rice and Paul Wolfowitz both visited the Bush home in Crawford, Texas, to advise candidate George W. Bush, center, on foreign policy.

living in Kosovo and Serbia, provinces in Yugoslavia.

Bush won the Iowa straw poll. A straw poll is an unofficial vote to gauge the popular opinion of a candidate or issue. The statewide straw poll in Iowa helps presidential candidates see where they stand at the beginning of their campaigns.

The press continued to play up Bush's mistakes. When asked about any previous drug use, Bush said that he could pass a background check for a White House appointee. Appointees had to have abstained from drug use for seven years. A *Dallas Morning News* headline read, "Bush Says He Hasn't Used Drugs in Last Seven Years." This, of course, was not what he had meant.

Then he said that he could pass the background check from when his father was president in 1989. That was taken to mean he had not used drugs for at least twenty-five years. Now the media wanted to know *when* George W. had used drugs, not *if* he had ever used them.

"I choose not to inventory my sins," Bush declared. He did not want to give out too many details about his younger days for fear that it would be a bad influence on future generations. He said he was afraid that kids would say, "'Well, the governor of Texas did it, why shouldn't I?'"[11] Instead of helping his cause, his explanation only made things worse. More rumors circulated about things he supposedly had done in his youth. George W. and Laura tried to laugh it off. "You have to—they're so silly," explained Laura.[12]

The New Hampshire primary caused an unwelcome surprise. Senator John McCain from Arizona defeated Bush. After the primary, Bush was angry and upset, but Laura calmed him down. "You've got to get out there, Bushie, and let people see that you're the better man for the job," Laura advised her husband.[13]

Bush's team came on stronger. He defeated McCain in South Carolina and then won more than enough votes in the remaining primaries to ensure his nomination at the Republican National Convention. Bush's father suggested that he consult with Richard B. Cheney for help in choosing a running mate.

George W. Bush and Cheney went to the Crawford,

Richard B. Cheney

In 1969 Cheney joined the Richard Nixon Administration. In 1974 Gerald Ford appointed Cheney the White House Chief of Staff and Assistant to the President. In 1977 Cheney was elected to Congress from Wyoming and became the Minority Whip in 1988. He helped the Minority Leader in the House of Representatives coordinate Republican responses to legislation.

Cheney served as Secretary of Defense from 1989 to 1993 and directed two large military efforts in Panama and in the Middle East. In 1991, he was awarded the Presidential Medal of Freedom, the nation's highest award given to a civilian. In 1995 Cheney became the Chairman and CEO of Halliburton, an energy equipment and construction company.[14]

Texas, ranch and, in the summer heat, discussed the possible choices for a running mate.

Colin Powell, everyone's first choice, had been the chairman of the Joint Chiefs of Staff during Operation Desert Storm. That is the highest military position that a person can achieve in the Department of Defense.[15] But Powell had to be ruled out because he was interested in becoming secretary of state. Also ruled out were former Missouri Senator John Danforth, New York governor George Pataki, and Senator John McCain. After a while, Cheney and Bush had cut most of the list.

Laura observed how well the two men got along. She asked her husband, "So why not pick Dick?"[16] Bush agreed. Dick Cheney seemed the perfect choice. He had been loyal to the Republican Party and had served George H.W. Bush well. He was not interested in running for president, so he would be totally focused on George W.'s agenda. The only drawback was that Cheney was sixty years old and had some health problems.

Now it was time to concentrate on Bush's opponent, Vice President Al Gore, the Democratic nominee for president. The October televised debates were approaching. Gore knew the issues well and was known to bring his own props to a debate. However, his stiff stance was a problem for many viewers. Whenever he tried to be "looser," it did not work.

Gore also had a tendency to overstate or exaggerate at times, and he had been caught doing it. For example, he once claimed to remember a lullaby he heard as a child, a song that had not come out until much later.[17]

Bush, on the other hand, had an easy style and he often used his good humor to advantage. But his tangled tongue still caused people to view him as unintelligent. "I don't think we need to be subliminable about the differences between our views on prescription drugs," Bush was quoted as saying. He meant to say "subliminal," but kept adding an extra syllable.[18]

That fall the poll numbers tightened, and the two candidates were neck-and-neck in the presidential race. The first debate was held in Boston, and neither man did well. Televised close-ups showed Gore sighing a lot, making him appear rude. Viewers also noticed Gore's orange skin, a result of bad makeup for television.

Bush did better in the second debate in Winston-Salem, North Carolina. But in the third debate, which was held in St. Louis, Missouri, he was again rather mediocre. For that last debate, the two candidates sat on stools and could move around the stage. At one point, Gore stood behind Bush and stared while Bush spoke. Once again, Gore's actions did not translate well for viewers. In the *San Francisco Chronicle* the next day, Mark Sandalow wrote, "George W. Bush may well have won last night's debate by not losing it."[19]

The polls were split almost evenly between the two candidates. Then, five days before the election, a Maine television station reported on Bush's drunk-driving arrest in Maine. This was the first time in almost twenty-five years that this issue had come up.

Most news organizations did not want to report something that might make them appear biased. Bush held a

Bush, left, and Al Gore, right, at the second debate. In the center is moderator Jim Lehrer.

press conference and admitted that he had been arrested for drunk driving. The news about the drunk-driving arrest did not appear to do much harm, thanks in part to the media's restraint.[20]

Tuesday, November 7, 2000, was Election Day. As the day progressed, it was obvious the election would be a close call. By dinnertime, Gore had 255 electoral votes, while Bush had 246.

Florida had twenty-five electoral votes, and the race there was too close to call. Whoever won the state of Florida would become the next president of the United States.

At 7:50 P.M., Eastern Standard Time, *CBS News* called the election for Gore, even though not all of the polls had closed in Florida. The Florida panhandle is in a different time zone, Central Standard Time. That area still had at least ten minutes of voting time left.

Just before 10 P.M. EST, the media declared that Florida was not yet decided, and withdrew Florida's electoral votes from Gore's column. The election was still undecided.

Electoral College

Delegates from each state, plus the District of Columbia, formally elect the president of the United States. The number of congressmen and senators in each state equals the number of delegates chosen to represent each state. These delegates, or electors, are chosen by popular vote. The candidate who has won the most votes in each state wins the elector's votes for that state. The electors cast the state's votes on the first Monday after the second Wednesday in December. The candidate must win 270 votes out of 538 votes in the Electoral College to become president of the United States.

Then, at 2:15 A.M. EST, Florida was called for Bush, with vote counters saying that he had enough electoral votes to win. Gore called to concede. But as the vote tallying in Florida continued, it became apparent that the election was still not over. Gore called back to retract his concession.

The media agreed with Gore, and withdrew its earlier announcement that Bush had won. Now the television networks were saying the race was too close to call. It would be another thirty-six days before a winner would be declared president in one of the closest races in U.S. history.

Bush watched the election returns with his parents, George and Barbara Bush, in Austin, Texas.

8
WHO WON?

ecause the vote was so close, Florida law required an automatic recount. A machine recount found Bush winning by a mere 327 votes, but Palm Beach and Volusia Counties started a hand recount. Both candidates filed lawsuits, raising the question of which ballots to count and which to discard.

On December 12, 2000, the U.S. Supreme Court voted 5–4 to stop the recount. The Justices decided that vote-counting standards varied too much from county to county and that there was not enough time for one official to oversee the entire recount.

Although he did not win the national popular vote, Bush had won Florida's electoral votes. That was enough to win the election. George W. Bush had become the president-elect of the United States. "I was not elected to

"BUSH PREVAILS," announced *The Express-Times* of Easton, Pennsylvania. Then, as the vote count narrowed, a later edition wondered, "PRESIDENT WHO?"

serve one party, but to serve one nation," said Bush. ". . . Whether you voted for me or not, I will do my best to serve your interests, and I will work to earn your respect."[1]

"Tonight, for the sake of the unity of our people and the strength of our democracy, I offer my concession," Gore said on December 13, 2000.[2]

Gore became one of four candidates to win the popular vote but lose the electoral vote, which determines the presidency. Andrew Jackson (1824), Samuel Tilden (1876), and Grover Cleveland (1888) had lost in the same way. Both Jackson and Cleveland went on to win the presidency four years after their losses.

There were many questions after the U.S. Supreme Court closed the election. Were all the ballots in Florida counted? Were minority voters discriminated against? A number of news organizations wanted to set straight who had actually won. *The New York Times*, *The Washington Post*, the Associated Press, and other media joined together to count the votes. *The Miami Herald* investigated on its own. During the recount, the press disagreed on whether to include the overvotes with the undervotes.

After months of ballot counting, *The New York Times* said that Bush would have won if the hand count of ballots had been completed in Florida.[3] Several months later, *The Miami Herald* agreed that Bush would have won.[4] But, they said, Gore would have won if the voting procedure had been perfect.[5]

The U.S. Department of Justice's civil rights division checked on allegations that

Overvotes vs. Undervotes

There were many voting irregularities in Florida. When a voter accidentally votes for more than one person, it is called an overvote. These ballots were discarded because of the difficulty in deciding voter intent.

An undervote is a voting card not punched all the way through. This causes "hanging chads" and "dimples." "Hanging chads" are the tiny pieces of paper that are not punched out all the way. One or two corners are still attached to the ballot. "Dimples" are indentations, where three or four corners are still attached.

Computer analysts began to recount the ballots in Fort Lauderdale, Florida.

Protesters gathered outside
the Supreme Court in
Washington, D.C.

minorities had been discriminated against
in the Florida election. After much investigation, the division's voting section
found that "the vast majority [of people calling to
complain]—over 95%—simply expressed opinions or
vented frustration about daily events in the ongoing
election dispute."[6]

George W. Bush was sworn into office on January 20,
2001. He launched immediately into his campaign agenda. During his first week in office, he introduced his
tax-cut plan and education plan to Congress. However, it
was not easy going.

The first hundred days are called the "honeymoon"
period with a new president, Congress, and the press.
But, because the election was so incredibly close and had

gone through so much legal wrangling, people were sharply divided.

When he was governor of Texas, Bush had bridged the differences between Democrats and Republicans. Washington, D.C., was a different story. Many Democrats believed the election was stolen from them.

Bush stayed focused on his agenda. He traveled to thirty states between March and May 2001, pushing his tax plan. The government had accumulated a large surplus of money, and Bush was worried that Congress would spend it frivolously.

Bush wanted to use the surplus to increase spending on education

Chief Justice William Rehnquist, right, administered the oath of office to President Bush, whose wife, Laura, and daughter Barbara stood at his side. Next to the Justice is former president Bill Clinton.

and defense, to pay down the national debt, and to cut taxes. Congress approved his plan, and his tax cut was signed into law in June 2001. This was his first domestic achievement.

Earlier, in April 2001, Bush was tested on the foreign front. A U.S. Navy patrol plane collided with a Chinese fighter jet over the South China Sea. The navy plane landed safely in the People's Republic of China. The Chinese fighter jet had been lost.[7]

Father and Son Presidents

Only once before had a son followed his father into the presidency. John Adams was our second president (1797–1801). His son John Quincy Adams ran against three men, none of whom had enough electoral votes to win. The House of Representatives selected John Quincy Adams to be our sixth president (1825–1829). Like George W. Bush, John Quincy Adams had not won the popular vote.

The accident had occurred over international airspace, so it should have ended there. China refused to release the American crewmembers and demanded a formal apology from the United States. "Our priorities are the prompt and safe return of the crew, and the return of the aircraft without further damaging or tampering," Bush said.[8]

After more meetings between the two countries, China agreed to release the Americans. However, it still retained the plane. The United States issued a formal apology on April 11, 2001, and the crew returned home. Three months later, China sent the dismantled surveillance plane back to the United States in two Russian cargo planes.[9] It marked the end of a tense diplomatic standoff. President Bush had handled the situation with calm diplomacy.

"He is doing very well with the public," said Andrew Kohut, director of the Pew Research Center for the People and the Press. "The China standoff was the number one story so far this year and he got strong approval there. And his tax proposal is being well recognized."[10]

That summer, President Bush was dealt a political blow. Vermont senator Jim Jeffords left the Republican Party and became an independent. Before Jeffords left, the U.S. Senate was divided. There were 50 Republicans and 50 Democrats, with the vice president having the tie-breaking vote.

Many moderate Republicans, like Jeffords, were uneasy with the size of the tax cuts. Democrats were unhappy, because the tax cuts meant reduced spending for social programs. Democrats and some Republicans feared the tax cuts would deplete the surplus. Jeffords had

Surplus vs. Deficit vs. Debt

The U.S. government receives money, called receipts, from taxes and other fees. The government also spends money, called outlay, on the military, Social Security and Medicare benefits, as well as other programs, such as medical research. When there are more receipts than outlay, there is a surplus. A deficit is when the outlay is more than receipts.

The U.S. Treasury borrows money when there is a deficit. The Treasury can borrow money by selling T-bills, notes, and savings bonds. This borrowed money becomes part of the total national debt. The debt is an accumulation of deficits.[11]

already often voted with the Democrats on many issues of taxes and spending. His personal beliefs and the more conservative Republican Party no longer meshed. Jeffords wanted to see more money available for a special-education fund.[12]

When Jeffords quit the Republican Party, the balance of power shifted to the Democrats. As an independent, Jeffords agreed to vote with the Democrats on all procedural matters. They rewarded him with the chairmanship of the Environment and Public Works Committee, a committee much less powerful than his old chairmanship.[13]

With the Democrats in control of the Senate, President Bush's initiatives were pushed aside. Some people questioned his leadership abilities as the first congressional session ended. He spent August at his ranch, with short trips around the country visiting his constituents. The summer ended with his approval rate climbing again.

9

THE DAY THAT CHANGED EVERYTHING

On the morning of September 11, 2001, President Bush was visiting Emma Booker Elementary in Sarasota, Florida. Just before his 9 A.M. arrival, he was told that a plane had plowed into the World Trade Center in New York City. It was first thought to be a small private plane. "What a horrible accident!" Bush said.[1]

He then called Condoleezza Rice, the National Security Advisor. A minute later, Bush walked into the second-grade classroom and listened to a reading exercise. At 9:07 A.M. Chief of Staff Andrew Card whispered in the president's ear. "A second plane hit the second tower. America is under attack." Card stepped away to avoid distrupting the class.[2] President Bush's face drained of color. Some people in the classroom noticed that his focus was not on the kids.[3] Six minutes later, Bush complimented the children on their reading.

Then he met with his staff, before speaking briefly to two hundred people who had gathered at the school. "Today we've had a national tragedy. Two airplanes have crashed into the World Trade Center in an apparent terrorist attack on our country," President Bush told the shocked crowd.[4]

While Bush was speaking, a third hijacked plane was headed for Washington, D.C. Secret Service agents barged into Vice President Cheney's office, grabbed Cheney under his arms, then hustled him to an underground bunker.

The third hijacked plane crashed into the Pentagon at 9:37 A.M. Meanwhile, Bush took off in Air Force One, the presidential plane. Cheney told him that it was not safe to return to the White House. The South Tower of the World Trade Center collapsed just before 10 A.M. A fourth hijacked plane crashed into a Pennsylvania field at 10:03 A.M. It had also been headed for Washington, D.C. No one knew how many planes might have been hijacked.

The Federal Aviation Administration grounded all air traffic to prevent more hijacking. This was the first time in history this order had been given. President Bush also gave an order to shoot down any planes that appeared to be controlled by terrorists.

Air Force One flew to Barksdale Air Force Base in

Louisiana. By the time they landed, the North Tower of the World Trade Center had also collapsed. The Louisiana stop was temporary, so that Bush could address the nation. "Freedom itself was attacked this morning by a faceless coward," he said.[5]

By this time, it was widely assumed that al Qaeda, a well-known terrorist organization, was behind the hijackings. The CIA had issued warnings about al Qaeda

"These acts shattered steel, but they cannot dent the steel of America's resolve," said President Bush in a speech to the nation on September 11, 2001.

and a possible attack, but there had been no concrete information on where or when.

Cheney and the Secret Service still did not feel it was safe for the president to return to the White House. So Air Force One flew to Offutt Air Force Base in Nebraska. This base had secure facilities, and Bush could meet with the National Security Council over a video link.

At the meeting, CIA Director George Tenet said that Osama bin Laden and al Qaeda appeared to be behind the attack. Three al Qaeda terrorists had been on the passenger list of the plane that had crashed into the Pentagon. "We're doing the assessment, but it looks like, it feels like, it smells like al Qaeda," he said.[6]

After the meeting, Bush flew to Washington, D.C. He decided it was time for the nation to see its leader back at work in the White House. He arrived at 7 P.M. and addressed the nation at 8:30 P.M. President Bush told America, "We will make no distinction between the terrorists who committed these acts and those who harbor them."[7]

After the speech, he once again met with the National Security Council and then with key advisers, who became his war cabinet. Secretary of State Colin Powell recommended that the U.S. go after Osama bin Laden in Afghanistan, where the Taliban rulers were harboring him and al Qaeda. Secretary of Defense Donald Rumsfeld wanted to go after all countries that supported terrorists.

In his diary that night, Bush wrote, "The Pearl Harbor of the 21st century took place today. We think it's Osama bin Laden. . . . We cannot allow a terrorist thug to hold us hostage."[8] By the next morning, the death count had climbed to more than three thousand. Bush wanted justice. "The deliberate and deadly attacks which were carried out yesterday against our country were more than acts of terror," he told reporters, "they were acts of war."[9]

Bush had to assemble an international coalition, which is an association of nations. Tony Blair, the British prime minister, had already pledged England's support. Russian president Vladimir Putin agreed to work with Bush to fight terrorism. President Bush also called the leaders of France, Germany, Canada, and China, but these leaders, although sympathetic to the victims, hesitated in their support of a vague war on terror. "My attitude all along was, if we have to go it alone, we'll go it alone; but I'd rather not," President Bush said. [10]

Al Qaeda and Osama bin Laden

Afghanistan's ruling party was the Taliban, Islamic rulers who took over the country after the Soviets left Afghanistan in 1992. Osama bin Laden, originally from Saudi Arabia, supported the Afghans who fought against the Soviet Union. Bin Laden's wealth provided financial aid, and he recruited extremist volunteers.

His guerrilla organization was called al Qaeda, which means "the camp" in Arabic. Al Qaeda members lived in caves and tents, hiding in the mountains.

After the Soviets left, bin Laden focused on the United States. In 1998, al Qaeda's declared mission was "to kill Americans and their allies." Bin Laden turned al Qaeda into a secret terrorist network.[11]

Bush met with the deputies of state, defense, the Joint Chiefs, the CIA, and the NSC. The deputies committee agreed that any war on terrorism would target Iraqi dictator Saddam Hussein, who was thought to be acquiring weapons of mass destruction. But their first concern was al Qaeda.

Pakistan, which borders Afghanistan, was also a concern because it recognized the Taliban as Afghanistan's official government. However, Pakistan agreed to support the United States in its war on terrorism.[12]

After the deputies committee meeting, Bush went to the Pentagon to study the damage. The next day, he visited the burn unit at Washington Hospital Center. On September 14, he spoke at Washington National Cathedral, leading four former presidents and the nation in prayer. "This nation is peaceful, but fierce when stirred to anger. This conflict was begun on the timing and terms of others. It will end in a way, and at an hour, of our choosing," he said.[13]

After the service, Bush flew to New York City. The smoke from the site of the World Trade Center could be smelled more than twenty-five miles away. Dust covered everything, and the streets were deserted. President Bush rode in a motorcade to Ground Zero, where the World Trade Center had stood only days ago. Along the route people waved flags and chanted, "USA! USA!"

Bush had not planned to speak, but a crowd of rescue workers greeted him. He reached for a bullhorn and

President Bush visited the site of the World Trade Center in New York City on September 14, 2001.

climbed on top of a wrecked fire truck. As he started to speak, a rescue worker shouted, "We can't hear you!"

"I can hear you," Bush replied. "The rest of the world hears you. And the people who knocked these buildings down will hear all of us soon."[14]

Then Bush visited Javits Center to speak to the victims' families. That weekend, Taliban leaders declared a holy war on the United States if the U.S. attacked Afghanistan.

On September 20, 2001, President Bush addressed the nation, speaking at a joint session of Congress. He announced the creation of the Office of Homeland Security to prevent terrorism on American soil. This independent agency would be accountable to the president. It would develop a national strategy to keep the United States safe from terrorist attacks. Some critics have complained that the agency invades the privacy of private citizens and restricts the freedoms of American citizens.

Eighty million Americans heard that speech. A professional hockey game in Philadelphia stopped so spectators could watch President Bush on the overhead screens. Bush's approval rating was the highest recorded in a Gallop Poll for a U.S. president.

With war come protesters. War protesters converged on Washington, D.C., San Francisco, New York City, and around the world. These people did not want the U.S. to retaliate with the military. They felt there were better, more peaceful ways to deal with the situation.

On October 7, President Bush announced "Operation Enduring Freedom." Its mission was to overthrow the Taliban regime in Afghanistan. The Taliban had steadfastly refused to turn over Osama bin Laden and continued to harbor al Qaeda members.

American and British forces bombed Kabul, Afghanistan's capital, as well as Kandahar, where the Taliban's supreme leader lived, and Jalalabad, where terrorists trained. Coalition forces destroyed al Qaeda's training camps and the Taliban's air defenses. Bin Laden escaped with key members of al Qaeda.

With the Taliban toppled and an interim government in place, Afghanistan lurched toward democracy. Terrorist attacks continued within the country, but the terrorists no longer ruled. On October 9, 2004, Afghanistan held its first free election. Women also voted for the first time.

Canada, Germany, Australia, and New Zealand sent troops to help the United States and the United Kingdom in Afghanistan. Italy, South Korea, Poland, and Spain also joined the coalition.

The Patriot Act

On October 26, 2001, six weeks after 9/11, the Patriot Act was signed into law. It gives U.S. law enforcement more authority to fight terrorism within the United States and overseas. The purpose of the act is to help find and prosecute terrorists. Critics worry that it threatens the civil liberties and privacy rights of American citizens and that the government cannot be held accountable. There have been some successful challenges to limit the Patriot Act. One section was ruled vague, and another was ruled unconstitutional. A revised Patriot Act was renewed by Congress in March 2006.

By January 2002, some semblance of normal politics
had returned to the United States, with Senate Majority
Leader Tom Daschle, a Democrat, complaining publicly
about Bush's tax cuts. In his State of the Union address
on January 29, 2002, Bush promised that the U.S. would
continue to "shut down terrorists camps, disrupt terrorists plans, and bring terrorists to justice."[15]

He called North Korea, Iran, and Iraq an "axis of
evil," and pledged to stop them from making weapons of
mass destruction while harboring terrorists. He promised
that the U.S. would keep fighting against terror until we
"see freedom's victory."[16]

In February and March 2002, UN inspectors found
Iraqi missiles with illegal range, and Iraq was ordered to
destroy them.[17] The United States, Britain, and Spain
wanted to use military force in Iraq, while France,
Germany, and Russia wanted intensified inspections.

Only the United States, Britain, Spain, and Bulgaria
supported the UN's using military force against Iraq.
Since Iraq had destroyed the illegal missiles, there were
not enough supporters in the UN for this plan.

Canada, Germany, New Zealand, and Pakistan were
against any military action in Iraq. Other countries, such
as Denmark, Romania, the Netherlands, and Ukraine,
did not send troops, but later became part of the peace-
keeping and reconstruction efforts.

In September 2002, Bush warned the UN that if it
would not take action in Iraq, then the U.S. would.

Congress authorized an attack on Iraq on October 11, 2002.

Through binoculars, President Bush looked out on North Korea, part of the "Axis of Evil."

UN inspectors found eleven empty chemical warheads southwest of Baghdad in early January 2003.[18] The Iraqis insisted the warheads were old and useless.

In his State of the Union address on January 28, 2003, President Bush declared, "All free nations have a stake in preventing sudden and catastrophic attacks."[19]

On March 17, 2003, Bush told Iraqi dictator Saddam Hussein to leave the country within forty-eight hours. When Hussein refused, "Operation Iraqi Freedom" began on March 20. By April 9, Basra had fallen to British forces, and Baghdad to the U.S. military.

All major fighting was over by April 14. On May 1, 2003, Bush flew to the deck of the aircraft carrier USS *Abraham Lincoln* to declare victory under a banner that said, "Mission Accomplished."

Strong Iraqi resistance continued to attack the coalition troops almost daily. In July 2003, Hussein's sons were killed, but Hussein had not been found.

Bush warned the UN that if it would not take action in Iraq, then the U.S. would.

The UN approved reconstruction efforts by the United States and Britain in October 2003. On December 13, U.S. soldiers found Hussein hiding in a hole.

In February 2004, Bush requested an independent commission study on U.S. intelligence-gathering techniques. The intelligence reports that Bush and British Prime Minister Tony Blair had used were considered to be seriously flawed. Meanwhile, Iraqi guerrilla forces were using suicide bombers to kill U.S. forces and were taking hostages, most of whom they killed.

In April 2004, the U.S. Army began an investigation into the abuses that had occurred at Abu Ghraib Prison in Iraq. Brigadier General Janis Karpinski was experienced in intelligence and operations, but not in running a prison. Most of those under her command also had little to no experience in handling prisoners. The soldiers mistreated, abused, and tortured prisoners. Photographs and videos were taken of the torture.

Specialist Joseph M. Darby was upset and outraged by the actions of the soldiers in the 372nd Military Police Company and reported the situation. Because of the resulting investigation, the Department of Defense charged seven soldiers with abuse of the prisoners; the seven were convicted in military court. Seventeen soldiers were removed from duty, and Karpinski was demoted in rank from brigadier general to colonel. Although the soldiers were punished, their actions caused an international scandal and damaged the credibility of the U.S. Army in Iraq.

In May 2004, Iraqi voters chose a prime minister and a president for the interim government. The United States returned power to Iraq's interim government at the end of June.

In 2004, President Bush was up for reelection. His Democratic opponent this time was Massachusetts Senator John Kerry.

Kerry was a decorated Vietnam War hero. After serving in Vietnam, Kerry had testified before Congress in 1971 against that war. This upset many Vietnam veterans. Kerry had originally voted for the war in Iraq, but soon became a vocal critic of the war.

When Kerry ran for president, he was a popular choice for those who opposed the war in Iraq. However, his positions on the Iraqi war, as well as the Vietnam War, once again angered a number of war veterans.

A group of Vietnam veterans produced several

Bush campaigned hard
for reelection.

television ads harshly critical of Kerry. They attacked his position on the Iraqi war, reminded viewers of his anti-Vietnam days, and questioned his courage under fire.

The *Washington Post* compared these allegations and the ones in a book by Vietnam war veteran John E. O'Neill to the information in another book about Kerry's Vietnam experiences based on his diaries. The claims on both sides had inconsistencies. The *Washington Post* concluded that the facts were not totally accurate on either partisan side.[20] The veterans' ads, though, still hurt the Democratic candidate.

Bush was ahead in the polls, until the fall debates. Kerry was an excellent debater, and many observers believed that he made the best showing in all three of the debates.

Once again the election came down to one state: This time it was Ohio, with its twenty electoral votes. On Election Day, November 2, 2004, the networks declined to predict a winner. By Wednesday afternoon, Bush had won Ohio. A few states' votes had not yet been counted, but the number of remaining electoral votes was not enough for Kerry to win.

At 2 P.M., Senator John Kerry addressed his supporters at Boston's Faneuil Hall. "Today I hope we can begin the healing," he said in his concession speech.[21]

With all the votes counted, President Bush had won 286 electoral votes and 51 percent of the popular vote. Senator Kerry had won 252 votes and 48 percent of the popular vote.

In his victory speech, President Bush said, "I will do all I can do to deserve your trust. A new term is a new opportunity to reach out to the whole nation."[22]

George W. Bush had done what his father had not been able to do. He had done what John Quincy Adams had not been able to do. He had won a second term in office, and it would be just as challenging as his first.

10

A TURBULENT WORLD

In January 2005, Iraqis voted for representatives to a General Assembly. The General Assembly would write their constitution. More than 8 million people voted, including women. It was Iraq's first free election. The United States military presence would remain in Iraq for peace-keeping and reconstruction duties.

The war in Iraq has been compared to the United States involvement in Vietnam, with its high casualty rate and vague goals. Bush's coalition had as many as thirty-eight countries in it at one time, all of them sending military assistance. But the number fell to twenty-four by 2005, and more people wanted to bring the troops home. "Our troops will come home when Iraq is capable of defending herself," Bush said.[1]

On an almost daily basis, terrorists within Iraq continued to try to stop the democratic process by senseless killings. President Bush's popularity in the polls was at an all-time low in 2005 as the situation in Iraq continued to drag on.

On August 29, 2005, Hurricane Katrina hit fifty-five miles east of New Orleans. A Category 5, with winds up to 175 miles per hour, as it crossed the Gulf of Mexico, it was downgraded to Category 3, with 125 mph winds, when it reached landfall. It caused devastating damage to the coasts of Louisiana, Mississippi, and Alabama, and killed at least 1,600 people. The city of New Orleans, which is below sea level, is surrounded by walls, called levees. The storm surge was twenty-five feet in places, overtopping the levees and washing out their foundations. Three of the levees around New Orleans breached—or broke—flooding 80 percent of the city. On September 8, 2005, President Bush called Hurricane Katrina "one of the worst natural disasters in our Nation's history."[2]

The 9/11 Commission Report

The 9/11 Commission investigated the September 11, 2001, attacks. "We have no credible evidence that Iraq and al Qaeda cooperated on attacks against the United States," the 9/11 Commission stated. The 9/11 Commission agreed that al Qaeda was responsible for other U.S. attacks, including the 1993 World Trade Center bombing, and would likely attack the U.S. again. It also concluded that intelligence gathered by the Central Intelligence Agency and the Federal Bureau of Investigation was either faulty or used incorrectly.[3] These conclusions were controversial.

Bush was heavily criticized for the federal government's response to Katrina, though others argued that local and state officials deserved just as much, if not more, of the blame. The president's words of encouragement for Michael Brown, head of the Federal Emergency Management Agency—"Brownie, you're doing a heck of a job"[4]—coupled with the horrific scenes televised from the Gulf Coast, left many Americans angry with the administration. Bush responded by visiting Louisiana and Mississippi repeatedly, and by proposing billions of dollars in federal aid to rebuild the stricken area.

A White House review of the crisis later concluded that Hurricane Katrina "necessitated a national response that

In an effort to boost people's spirits, in September 2005 President Bush toured many communities devastated by Hurricane Katrina. This neighborhood is in Biloxi, Mississippi.

Federal, State, and local officials were unprepared to provide. . . . The Federal response suffered from significant organization and coordination problems during this week of crisis. . . . [These are not problems] that began and ended with Hurricane Katrina."[5]

On December 15, 2005, Iraqis went to their polls to vote. This resulted in their first permanent government since Hussein had been overthrown. Lieutenant General John R. Vines said that in 2005, "a new Iraq was born."[6] The Iraqis had three elections and approved a new constitution. "It was the most liberal constitution in the Islamic world," Vines commented after he returned home with 18th Airborne Corps.[7]

The Iraqis still needed help with training and reconstruction. Cheney said, "As the Iraqi forces gain strength and experience, and as the political process advances, we'll be able to decrease troop levels without losing our capacity to defeat the terrorists."[8]

Since the war in Iraq began, there had been rumors that there would be a civil war. In February 2006, when the Shiite Golden Mosque was bombed, a wave of violence followed. The Golden Mosque is revered because it is the resting place for three of Mohammed's descendants. Many Shiites, as well as the Iranian president, Mahmoud Ahmadinejad, blamed the United States and Israel, as well as Sunnis, for the attack in Samarra. Angry Shiites bombed Sunni mosques and killed many people.[9]

The Iraqi security forces responded to the violence,

with help from the coalition forces, and got it under control. U.S. Army General George W. Casey, who is the commander of the Multi-National Force in Iraq, said, "It appears that the crisis has passed." He felt the Iraqi security forces did "generally well" and that investigations were under way. He said he believed that al Qaeda was involved.[10]

"The people of Iraq are uniting against the insurgency," said Army Major General Rick Lynch. "Out in al Anbar, the terrorists and foreign fighters have become the enemy to the people."[11]

Iraqi reconstruction cost a lot of money, money that President Bush had to fight for in Congress. The proposed budget for 2007 was lean and would try to hold down all nondefense spending. The Republican-controlled Congress had rejected many spending restraints that President Bush had proposed before.

From the war in Iraq, President Bush intended to move to the war on Capitol Hill with Congress. "To keep our economy growing and our small-business sector strong," Bush said, "we need to ensure that you keep more of what you can—so Congress needs to make the tax cuts permanent."[12]

Many members of Congress blamed President Bush and his earlier tax cuts for using up the budget surplus. Some felt the tax cuts were responsible for the huge deficit.

The top economist at the International Monetary

Fund, Raghuram Rajan, expressed his worry that the United States economy was in serious trouble. He feared that the government had not been disciplined in its financial affairs.[13] The deficit for 2006 could top $400 billion. Some of the spending went into relief efforts along the Gulf Coast where hurricane damage was extensive in 2005. Still, Bush vowed that the deficit would be cut in half by 2009.[14]

The Center on Budget and Policy Priorities studied the effectiveness of the tax cuts from 2001, 2002, and 2003. It is a nonprofit, nonpartisan research organization. The center found that the tax cuts were not effective in stimulating the weak economy. It also found that increased interest payments on the debt would be more than $1.1 trillion.[15]

Peter Ferrara, director of the International Center for Law and Economics, said, "When you want to stimulate the economy you run bigger deficits which pump up the demand for goods and services, leading to greater output." When the budget deficit is reduced, it drags down the economy. This theory, Keynesian economics, "is still taught in our colleges and universities as the foundation of macroeconomic theory," Ferrara pointed out, "and most practicing economists still think of it that way." The right kind of tax cuts would motive people to save and to invest, stimulating the economy.[16]

Claims for unemployment benefits fell in March 2006, as measured by the Labor Department. Patrick

Fearon is a senior economist with A. G. Edwards & Sons. Commenting on the fall in jobless claims, Fearon said, "Initial claims [have been] really pretty low compared with the size of the workforce and the size of the economy."[17]

"It is more good news for the economy," said Michael Englund, the chief economist at Action Economics. "The market should be bracing for another strong payroll report in March [2006]."[18]

> The **right** kind of **tax cuts** would **motive** people to save and to **invest**, stimulating the **economy**.

Ultimately, time will tell what effect President Bush's tax cuts have on the economy. But by spring 2006, the results of the tax cuts and high deficit were making some people nervous, so some of Bush's domestic reforms were postponed.

Social Security was one of those reforms. President Bush wanted to make sure that Social Security had a solid foundation. While it is fine for today's seniors, its foundation of support is growing smaller. Today's seniors receive Social Security benefits that come from the earnings of a smaller number of workers.

So that benefits would not be cut for the next generation, Bush wanted to privatize Social Security. That would have allowed workers to invest the money today and save it for their retirement in private accounts. Many feared that this was too radical a change and worried that some of the elderly would wind up with no financial help at all.

Bush's plan to change Social Security—always considered politically difficult—languished. The president said it was because he had had to use all of his clout to support the war in Iraq. "Social Security—it didn't get done," the president said.[19] Meanwhile, a Bush-supported prescription drug benefit for older Americans under Medicare was controversial, with its critics concerned that it was costly and confusing.

Bush's education reforms were slated to have a healthy budget increase for 2007. Since taking office, President Bush had increased the funding for education by 33 percent. Early results of the No Child Left Behind Act (NCLB) that Bush signed on January 8, 2002, had shown it to be successful so far.

The Center on Education Policy (CEP) is a national, independent advocate for public education. In November 2005, CEP said that restructuring of struggling schools showed promising results. Restructuring is the last step that NCLB provides for schools that have not shown improvement. The progress of 133 schools in Michigan had been tracked for a number of years. These mostly urban schools had not met the Adequate Yearly Progress (AYP) that NCLB requires. After restructuring, 113 of the schools improved test scores and made AYP. Still, this does not

Promoting the No Child Left Behind Act, President and Mrs. Bush visited this school in Glen Burnie, Maryland. At left is fifth-grade teacher Laneie Taylor.

mean that restructuring is a miracle cure. These encouraging results could also have resulted from a combination of reforms.[20] The full impact of NCLB would not be seen for a few more years, as restructuring continued for failing schools.

The year 2005 brought changes to the Supreme Court. There are eight Associate Justices and one Chief Justice who are appointed to their positions for life. When there is an opening, a president nominates a candidate, who then must be approved by the Senate.

Associate Justice Sandra Day O'Connor announced her retirement in July 2005, and President Bush nominated John Roberts to replace her. When Chief Justice William Rehnquist died in September, Bush withdrew his nomination of Roberts as O'Connor's replacement.

Instead, he nominated John Roberts to be Rehnquist's successor as chief justice. There was some opposition from the Democrats, but Roberts's nomination was approved by the Senate Judiciary Committee, 13–5. The full Senate confirmed Roberts's nomination on September 29, 2005 with a vote of 78–22.

Bush asked Helen Miers to head the committee searching for someone to replace O'Connor. Democrat Harry Reid, who is the Senate Minority Leader, recommended that O'Connor's replacement be Miers. On October 3, 2005, Bush nominated Miers to be an Associate Justice. Her nomination was widely criticized by both Republicans and Democrats because of her lack of experience, and by conservatives who doubted that she would rule in their favor on abortion and other issues.

By the end of the month, Miers asked that her nomination be withdrawn and Bush reluctantly accepted it. In her place, Bush nominated Samuel Alito. Although environmentalists and gun-control lobbies were opposed to Alito, he was confirmed as an Associate Justice in January 2006.

The Dubai Ports deal in February and March 2006 caused an uproar. DP World is a port operator which manages the commercial and operational aspects of ports through Dubai Ports World (DPW). DPW is owned by the United Arab Emirates (UAE) government. In November 2005 they offered to buy all of the stock of the P&O Group, a privately owned British shipping firm.

P&O had been managing six U.S. East Coast ports, but with its acquisition, DPW would take over.

Even though UAE is portrayed as friendly to the United States, most Americans felt very uneasy about the idea of having an Arab country manage what goes through U.S. ports. A press release from the Department of Homeland Security explained that DP World would operate and manage only certain individual terminals located within six U.S. ports. This, however, was not enough reassurance to the American public, who were still remembering 9/11.

The House of Representatives voted to block the DPW deal. Although Bush had been in favor of the deal, DP World decided to back out in view of all the negative publicity. Because Bush had been in favor of the deal, his popularity dropped again.

George W. Bush's presidency has been buffeted by all sorts of tempests— literally, in Katrina's case, but also by devastating attacks by al Qaeda and by many controversies. How does Bush feel about being president in such a turbulent world? "I love my job," he told the guests at a dinner back in May 2001.[21]

Several years later, at an event in Dayton, Ohio, in May 2004, George W. was asked the same question. After all the crises and challenges, he could still repeat the sentiment. "I love my job," said George Walker Bush.[22]

President Bush is ready to take on new challenges.

CHRONOLOGY

1946   George Walker Bush is born July 6 in New Haven, Connecticut.

1948   Bush family moves to Odessa, Texas.

1949   Family moves to California.

1950   Bush family moves to Midland, Texas.

1953   Three-year-old sister Robin becomes ill with leukemia and dies.

1959   Bush family moves to Houston, Texas.

1961   George W. starts tenth grade at Phillips Academy in Andover, Massachusetts.

1964   Begins college at Yale University in New Haven, Connecticut. Helps in his father's race for U.S. Senate, but the elder Bush loses the election.

1966   Helps his father run for Congress, and this time he is elected.

1968   Graduates from Yale University with a degree in history. Joins the Texas Air National Guard to become a pilot.

1970   Graduates from Combat Crew Training School and is stationed at Ellington Air Force Base in Houston, Texas.

1972   Transfers to Alabama unit of National Guard so he can work on Winton Blount's Senate campaign.

1973   Transfers back to Houston and becomes a mentor in Professionals United for Leadership (PULL). Texas Air National Guard transfers George W. to Boston unit so he can attend Harvard Business School. Receives early release from National Guard.

Graduates from Harvard with master's degree in business administration. Moves back to Midland, Texas, to become a land man in the oil industry.	**1975**
Starts his own company, Arbusto Energy, Inc.	**1976**
Meets librarian Laura Welch and marries her three months later, on November 5.	**1977**
Runs for a seat in Congress, but loses the election.	**1978**
His father is elected vice president of the United States.	**1980**
Arbusto Energy, Inc., is renamed Bush Exploration. Twin daughters Jenna and Barbara Bush are born on November 25.	**1981**
Father is reelected vice president of the United States. Bush Exploration merges with Spectrum 7 Energy Corporation.	**1984**
Harken Energy Corporation takes over Spectrum 7.	**1986**
Father is elected president of the United States.	**1988**
George W. forms a partnership to purchase the Texas Rangers baseball team.	**1989**
Father loses reelection bid for president of the United States.	**1992**
George W. runs for governor of Texas against incumbent Ann Richards and wins.	**1994**
George W. wins reelection as Texas governor. Sells his shares of Texas Rangers. Decides to run for president of the United States against vice president Al Gore.	**1998**
Elected president of the United States.	**2000**

2001   Terrorists attack the United States on September 11, killing thousands. Operation Enduring Freedom takes down the Taliban regime of Afghanistan, but Osama bin Laden and members of al Qaeda escape.

2002   No Child Left Behind Act is signed into law. Iraq is suspected of having weapons of mass destruction and cooperating with al Qaeda.

2003   Operation Iraqi Freedom topples Saddam Hussein's dictatorship in Iraq.

2004   Bush wins reelection to another term as president, running against Senator John Kerry.

2005   Iraq holds its first free election, and women vote for the first time. President Bush appoints two Supreme Court Justices, and the Senate confirms them.

2006   The Shiite Golden Mosque was bombed and al Qaeda is suspected. The Dubai Ports deal with the United Arab Emirates is blocked by Congress. Rate of unemployment is going steadily down.

CHAPTER NOTES

Chapter 1. Running for Office

1. Christopher Andersen, *George and Laura: Portrait of an American Marriage* (New York: HarperCollins Publishers, 2002), p. 119.

2. Trilateral Commission Web site <http://www.trilateral.org/> (February 20, 2006).

3. Andersen, p. 128.

4. Lois Romano and George Lardner Jr., "Young Bush, A Political Natural, Revs Up," *Washington Post*, July 29, 1999, p. A1.

5. Ibid.

6. Ibid.

7. Patricia Kilday Hart, "Not So Great in '78," *Texas Monthly*, June 1999, p. 111.

8. Romano and Lardner Jr., p. A1.

9. Hart, p. 139.

10. Ibid.

11. Bill Minutaglio, *First Son: George W. Bush and the Bush Family Dynasty* (New York: Three Rivers Press, 1999), p. 193.

Chapter 2. Growing Up in Midland, Texas

1. "Leukemia," MedicineNet.com <http://www.medicinenet. com/leukemia/article.htm> (February 20, 2006).

2. Barbara Bush, *A Memoir* (New York: Charles Scribner's Sons, 1994), p. 44.

3. George Lardner Jr. and Lois Romano, "In His Own Words: 'I Remember the Sadness,'" *Washington Post*, July 26, 1999, p. A11.

4. George Bush, *A Charge to Keep* (New York: William Morrow and Company, 1999), p. 14.

5. Barbara Bush, *A Memoir*, p. 47.

6. George Bush, *A Charge to Keep*, p. 19.

7. Lois Romano and George Lardner Jr., "Bush: So-So Student but a Campus Mover," *Washington Post*, July 27, 1999, p. A1.

8. Ibid.

9. Barbara Bush, *A Memoir*, p. 56.

10. George Bush, *A Charge to Keep*, p. 20.

11. Ibid., pp. 20–22.

Chapter 3. College and the National Guard

1. Lois Romano and George Lardner Jr., "Bush: So-So Student but a Campus Mover," *Washington Post*, July 27, 1999, p. A1.

2. Helen Thorpe, "Go East, Young Man," *Texas Monthly*, June 1999, p. 132.

3. Christopher Andersen, *George and Laura: Portrait of an American Marriage* (New York: HarperCollins, 2002), p. 60.

4. Thorpe, p. 132.

5. Ronald Kessler, *A Matter of Character: Inside the White House of George W. Bush* (New York: Sentinel/Penguin Group, 2004), p. 31.

6. George W. Bush, *A Charge to Keep* (New York: William Morrow and Company, 1999), p. 47.

7. Andersen, p. 70.

8. Bill Minutaglio, *First Son: George W. Bush and the Bush Family Dynasty* (New York: Three Rivers Press, 1999), p. 90.

9. Ibid.

10. Andersen, p. 73.

11. Robert K. Brigham and E. Kenneth Hoffman, "Battlefield Vietnam: A Brief History," <http:www.pbs.org/battlefieldvietnam/history/index.html> (February 20, 2006).

12. Bush, *A Charge to Keep*, p. 50.

13. Minutaglio, p. 121.

14. George Lardner Jr. and Lois Romano, "At Height of Vietnam, Bush Picks Guard," *Washington Post*, July 28, 1999, p. A1.

15. Minutaglio, p. 122.

16. Ibid., p. 121.

17. Skip Hollandsworth, "Younger. Wilder?" *Texas Monthly*, June 1999, p. 108.

18. Minutaglio, p. 139.

19. Frank Bruni, *Ambling into History* (New York: HarperCollins Publishers, 2002), p. 139.

20. Kessler, p. 35.

21. Lardner Jr. and Romano, p. A1.

22. Ibid.

23. Hollandsworth, p. 110.

24. Lardner Jr. and Romano, p. A1.

25. Bush, *A Charge to Keep*, p. 60.

Chapter 4. The Oil Business—Boom to Bust

1. George W. Bush, *A Charge to Keep* (New York: William Morrow and Company, 1999), p. 61.

2. Ronald Kessler, *A Matter of Character: Inside the White House of George W. Bush* (New York: Sentinel/Penguin Group, 2004), p. 40.

3. George Lardner Jr. and Lois Romano, "Bush Name Helps Fuel Oil Dealings," *Washington Post*, July 30, 1999, p. A1.

4. Bush, *A Charge to Keep*, p. 79.

5. Ibid., p. 81.

6. Ibid.

7. Barbara Bush, *A Memoir* (New York: Charles Scribner's Sons, 1994), p. 140.

8. Bush, *A Charge to Keep*, p. 63.

9. Michael E. Williams, Ph.D. (University of Denver), and Michael Brandl, Ph.D. (University of Texas at Austin), "The First National Bank of Midland Bank Failure: A Historical Perspective," April 2000, p. 10 <http://www.mccombs.utexas.edu/faculty/michael.brandl/FNBM%20paperIV.doc> (February 20, 2006).

10. Ibid., pp. 1–2.

11. Ibid., p. 2.

12. FDIC Web site <http://www.fdic.gov/> (February 20, 2006).

13. "Oil Price History and Analysis," *Energy Economist Newsletter*, WTRG Economics <http://www.wtrg.com/prices.htm> (February 20, 2006).

14. David Brown, "Crash of '86 Left Permanent Scars: New Mindset Born of Pain," Oil Crash Remembered series, American Association of Petroleum Geologist Explorer Magazine, January 2006 <http://www.aapg.org/explorer/2006/01jan/crash.cfm> (February 20, 2006).

15. Lardner Jr. and Romano, "Bush Name Helps Fuel Oil Dealings," p. A1.

16. Ibid.

17. Bush, *A Charge to Keep*, p. 133.

18. Lois Romano and George Lardner Jr., "Bush's Life-Changing Year," *Washington Post*, July 25, 1999, p. A1.

19. "Symptoms of Alcoholism," Health Topics, University of Iowa, Hospitals & Clinics/University of Iowa Health Care <http://www. uihealthcare.com/topics/alcoholproblems/alco4137.html> (February 20, 2006).

20. "Signs and Symptoms of Alcoholism," <http://wy.essortment.com/ alcoholismsympt_rcpn.htm> (February 20, 2006).

21. Christopher Andersen, *George and Laura: Portrait of an American Marriage* (New York: HarperCollins, 2002), pp. 144–145

22. Bush, *A Charge to Keep*, p. 136.

23. Kessler, p. 48.

24. "George W. Bush" <http://www.usa-presidents.info/gwbush.htm>

25. Bush, *A Charge to Keep*, p. 139.

Chapter 5. Politics and Baseball

1. Christopher Andersen, *George and Laura: Portrait of an American Marriage* (New York: HarperCollins, 2002), p. 152.

2. Paul Burka, "The W. Nobody Knows," *Texas Monthly*, June 1999, p. 115.

3. George W. Bush, *A Charge to Keep* (New York: William Morrow, 1999), p. 178.

4. Evan Smith, "George, Washington," *Texas Monthly*, June 1999, p. 144.

5. Andersen, p. 154.

6. Smith, p. 111.

7. Barbara Bush, *A Memoir* (New York: Charles Scribner's Sons, 1994), p. 238.

8. George W. Bush, *A Charge to Keep*, p. 198.

9. Barbara Bush, *A Memoir*, p. 290.

10. Ronald Kessler, *A Matter of Character: Inside the White House of George W. Bush* (New York: Sentinel, 2004), p. 54.

11. "Bahrain," The World Factbook, updated February 10, 2005 <http://www.cia.gov/cia/publications/factbook/geos/ba.html>

12. George Lardner Jr., "The Harken-Bahrain Deal: A Baseless Suspicion," *Washington Post*, July 30, 1999, p. A20.

13. Ibid.

14. George Lardner Jr., and Lois Romano, "Bush Name Helps Fuel Oil Dealings," *Washington Post*, July 30, 1999, p. A1.

15. Ibid.

Chapter 6. The Governor's Race

1. Ronald Kessler, *A Matter of Character: Inside the White House of George W. Bush* (New York: Sentinel/Penguin Group, 2004), p. 54.

2. Lois Romano and George Lardner Jr., "Bush's Move Up to the Majors," *Washington Post*, July 31, 1999, Page A1.

3. Kessler, p. 54.

4. George W. Bush, *A Charge to Keep* (New York: William Morrow, 1999), p. 24.

5. Romano and Lardner Jr., "Bush's Move Up to the Majors," p. A1.

6. Dan Balz, "Team Bush: The Iron Triangle," *Washington Post*, July 23, 1999, p. C1.

7. Bush, *A Charge to Keep*, p. 34.

8. Ibid., p. 37.

9. Ibid., p. 38.

10. Christopher Andersen, *George and Laura: Portrait of an American Marriage* (New York: HarperCollins, 2002), p. 173.

11. Ibid., p. 172.

12. Ibid., p. 179.

13. Kessler, p. 60.

14. Karla Faye Tucker, letter to Governor George W. Bush, reprinted in the *Houston Chronicle*, January 20, 1998, p. 1.

15. Ibid.

16. Joseph Geringer, "Karla Faye Tucker: Texas' Controversial Murderess," Court TV's Crime Library; viewed at <http://www.crimelibrary.com/notorious_murders/women/tucker.1.html> (February 20, 2006).

17. Bush, *A Charge to Keep*, p. 150.

18. Ibid., pp. 150–154.

Chapter 7. Running for the Big Prize

1. Christopher Andersen, *George and Laura: Portrait of an American Marriage* (New York: HarperCollins, 2002), p. 194.

2. "Texas Legislature," Alamo Community College District; viewed at Web site <http://www.accd.edu/sac/gov/berrier/2301/legislature.htm> (February 20, 2006).

3. Thomas M. Freiling, ed., *George W. Bush on God and Country* (Washington, D.C.: Allegiance Press, 2004), p. 27.

4. Frank Bruni, *Ambling into History: The Unlikely Odyssey of George W. Bush* (New York: Perennial/HarperCollins, 2002), p. 55.

5. Ibid. pp. 40–41.

6. Ibid., p. 57.

7. Ibid., p. 50.

8. Ibid., p. 52.

9. Kelly Wallace, "President-Elect Touted by Staff as a Seasoned World Traveler," CNN.com, December 17, 2000 <http://archives.cnn.com/2000/ALLPOLITICS/stories/12/17/bush.world.traveler> (February 20, 2006).

10. Andersen, p. 209.

11. Ibid., pp. 210–211.

12. Ibid., p. 212.

13. Ibid.

14. "Richard B. Cheney, Vice President," The White House Web site, <http://www.whitehouse.gov/vicepresident/> (February 20, 2006).

15. "Secretary of State Colin L. Powell," The White House Web site, <http://www.whitehouse.gov/government/powell-bio.html> (February 20, 2006).

16. Andersen, p. 218.

17. Eric Engberg, "Your Guide to 'Bush vs. Gore,'" CBS News Web site, October 2, 2000 <http://www.cbsnews.com/stories/2000/10/02/politics/printable237855.shtml> (February 20, 2006).

18. Ibid.

19. Bruni, p. 188.

20. Ibid., pp. 193–194.

Chapter 8. Who Won?

1. Matt Smith, "Bush: I Will Work to Earn Your Respect," December 13, 2000, Cnn.com, Election 2000, <http://archives.cnn.com/2000/ALLPOLITICS/stories/12/13/bush.ends.campaign/index.html> (February 20, 2006).

2. "Gore Concedes Presidential Election," Election 2000, CNN.com, December 13, 2000, <http://archives.cnn.com/2000/ ALLPOLITICS/stories/12/13/gore.ends.campaign/index.html> (February 20, 2006).

3. Ford Fessenden and John M. Broder, "Study of Disputed Florida Ballots Finds Justices Did Not Cast the Deciding Vote," *The New York Times*, November 12, 2001, p. A18.

4. Martin Merzer, "Review Shows Ballots Say Bush," *The Miami Herald*, April 4, 2001, p. A4.

5. Anabelle de Gale, Lila Arzula, and Curtis Morgan, "If the Vote Were Flawless . . . Gore Would Have Had the Edge in Glitch-Free Florida Balloting, Based on a Herald Analysis," *The Miami Herald*, March 31, 2001, p. A4.

6. Ralph F. Boyd Jr., Assistant Attorney General, U.S. Department of Justice, Civil Rights Division, letter to the Honorable Patrick Leahy, Chairman, Committee on the Judiciary, United States Senate, June 7, 2002.

7. "Chinese Jets Intercept U.S. Navy Plane," CNN.com/World, April 1, 2001, <http://archives.cnn.com/2001/WORLD/asiapcf/east/04/01/china.usnavy> (February 20, 2006).

8. "President Bush's Statement," Online NewsHour, April 11, 2001 <http://www.pbs.org/newshour/bb/asia/china/plane/bush_4-11.html> (February 20, 2006).

9. "Recovery of American Spy Plane Begins in China," Online NewsHour, June 15, 2001 <http://www.pbs.org/newshour/updates/june01/china_6-15.html> (February 20, 2006).

10. "President Bush's First 100 Days: Political Wrap," Online NewsHour, April 27, 2001 <http://www.pbs.org/newshour/shields&gigot/april01/sg_4-27.html> (February 20, 2006).

11. "Debt versus Deficit: What's the Difference?," Bureau of the Public Debt, United States Department of the Treasury, <http://www.publicdebt.treas.gov/bpd/bpd08052004.htm> (February 20, 2006).

12. "Senator Jeffords' Party Change a Result of a Dispute over Funding for the Disabled," Editorials, *New Horizons Un-Limited Inc.*, July 27, 2001 <http://www.new-horizons.org/elgjef.html> (January 10, 2006).

13. John Lancaster and Helen Dewar, "Jeffords Tips Senate Power," *Washington Post*, Friday, May 25, 2001, p. A01.

Chapter 9. The Day That Changed Everything

1. Sharon Churcher, "The Day the President Went Missing," *The Daily Mail*, September 8, 2002.

2. Robert Plunket, "The President in Sarasota," *Sarasota Magazine,* November 2001 <http://www.sarasotamagazine.com/ pages/hotstories/hotstories.asp?136> (March 10, 2006).

3. Andrew Card, "9/11 Voices: What If You Had to Tell The President?" *San Francisco Chronicle,* September 11, 2002, <http://sfgate.com/cgi-bin/article.cgi?f=/c/a/2002/09/11/ MN911voice03.DTL> (March 10, 2006).

4. President George W. Bush, "Remarks by the President After Two Planes Crashed Into World Trade Center," Emma Booker Elementary School, Sarasota, Florida, September 11, 2001, <http://www.whitehouse.gov/news/releases/2001/09/20010911.html> (March 10, 2006).

5. David E. Sanger and Don Van Natta Jr., "In Four Days, A National Crisis Changes Bush's Presidency," *The New York Times,* September 16, 2001.

6. Quoted in "The President's Story," CBSNews.com, September 10, 2003, <http://www.cbsnews.com/stories/2002/09/11/60II/521718.shtml> (March 10, 2006).

7. George W. Bush, "Statement by the President in His Address to the Nation," White House, Washington, D.C.

8. Dan Balz and Bob Woodward, "10 Days in September: America's Chaotic Road to War," *Washington Post,* January 27, 2002, p. A1.

9. "The President's Story: Part II, The Days After," CBSNews.com, September 10, 2003, <http://www.cbsnews.com/stories/2002/09/11/60II521684.shtml> (February 20, 2006).

10. Bob Woodward and Dan Balz, "10 Days in September: 'We Will Rally the World,'" *Washington Post,* January 28, 2002, p. A1.

11. Tom Gielten, B.A., M.Ed., "September 11 Attacks," Microsoft Encarta 2004 <http://encarta.msn.com/text_ 701509060__1/September _11_Attacks.html> (March 10, 2006).

12. Woodward and Balz, "10 Days in September: 'We Will Rally the World.'"

13. Thomas M. Freiling, ed., *George W. Bush on God and Country,* (Washington, D.C.: Allegiance Press, 2004), p. 111.

14. David Frum, *The Right Man: The Surprise Presidency of George W. Bush* (New York: Random House, 2003), p 140.

15. George W. Bush, "President Delivers State of the Union Address," United States Capitol, Washington, D.C., January 29, 2002.

16. Ibid.

17. "Iraqi Warheads and Tougher Talk," CNN.com, WORLD, January 16, 2003 <http://www.cnn.com/2003/WORLD/meast/01/16/sproject.irq.wrap/> (February 20, 2006).

18. "NTI: Country Overviews: Iraq: Missile Import/Export," Nuclear Threat Initiative Web site <http://www.nti.org/e_research/profiles/Iran/Missile/2970_2421.html> (February 20, 2006).

19. George W. Bush, "President Delivers 'State of the Union,'" United States Capitol, Washington, D.C., January 28, 2003.

20. Michael Dobbs, "Swift Boat Account Incomplete," *Washington Post*, August 22, 2004, p. A1.

21. John Kerry, "Transcript of John Kerry's Concession Speech," *The New York Times*, November 3, 2004, nytimes.com Web site <http://www.nytimes.com/2004/11/03/politics/campaign/03cnd-kerry-text.html> (February 20, 2006).

22. Dan Balz, "Bush Wins Second Term," *Washington Post*, November 4, 2004, p. A1.

Chapter 10. A Turbulent World

1. President's Press Conference, James S. Brady Briefing Room, March 16, 2005, Office of the Press Secretary, the White House <http://www.whitehouse.gov/news/releases/2005/03/20050316-3.html> (March 20, 2006).

2. Mike Brunker, "9/11 Panel Sees No Link Between Iraq, al-Qaida," MSNBC.com, 6:48 p.m. ET, June 16, 2004 <http://www.msnbc.msn.com/id/5223932> (March 20, 2006).

3. George W. Bush, September 8, 2005, <http://www.whitehouse.gov/reports/katrina-lessons-learned/chapter1.html> (April 17, 2005).

4. Jennifer Loven, "Day after Day, Bush White House Trying to Regain Its Footing and Repair Its Image" Associated Press, September 6, 2005.

5. The White House, "Katrina in Perspective: Conclusion," <http://www.whitehouse.gov/reports/katrina-lessons-learned/chapter4.html> (April 17, 2005).

6. "N.C. General Leads Troops Home From Duty in Iraq," Associated Press, Journalnow.com, online partner of the *Winston-Salem Journal*, January 23, 2006 <http://www.journalnow.com/servlet/ Satellite?pagename=WSJ%2FM> (March 20, 2006).

7. Ibid.

8. Steve Holland, "US Troops Face Another Three Years in Iraq," Independent Online, March 21, 2006 <http://www.int.iol.co.za/general news/newsprint.php?art_id=qw1142> (March 20, 2006).

9. Mary Crane, "Fears of Civil War Follow Golden Mosque Attack," Council on Foreign Relations, February 23, 2006 <http://www.cfr.org/ publication/9931/fears_of_civil_war_follow_golden_mosque_attack.html> (March 20, 2006).

10. Ann Scott Tyson, "U.S. Commander in Iraq Says 'Crisis Has Passed,'" *Washington Post*, March 4, 2006, <http: www.washingtonpost. com/wp-dyn/content/article/2006/03/03/ AR2006030300767_pf.html> (March 20, 2006).

11. Samantha L. Quigley, "Iraqis Fed Up with Insurgency, General Says," United States Department of Defense news articles, March 9, 2006 <http://www.defenselink.mil/news/Mar2006/20060309_4433.html> (March 20, 2006).

12. Joel Havemann and Janet Hook, "A Budget with Bold on Hold," *Los Angeles Times*, January 22, 2006 <http://www.latimes.com/news/politics/ la-na-budget22jan22,0,56867461.story?coll= la=headlines-politics> (March 20, 2006).

13. Alex Brummer, "Fears Grow for US Economy," *The Daily Mail*, January 12, 2006, on thisismoney.com.uk Web site <http://www. thisismoney.co.uk/news/article.html?in_article_id=406208&in_ page_id=19&in> (March 20, 2006).

14. Martin Crutsinger (The Associated Press), "Corporate Taxes, Gov't Spending Hit Records," *Washington Post*, July 12, 2006, <http:// www.washingtonpost.com/wp-dyn/content/article/2006/01/12/ AR2006011201143_pf.htm> (March 20, 2006).

15. "Tax Returns: New Report Questions Effectiveness, Design of Bush Tax Cuts through 2004 and Beyond," Press Release from the Center on Budget and Policy Priorities, Friday, April 23, 2004 <http://www.cbpp.org/ 4-14-04tax-pr.htm> (March 20, 2006).

16. Peter Ferrara, "The Tax-Cut Critics," Guest Comment, National Review Online, May 20, 2003 <http:www.nationalreview. com/nrof_ comment/comment-ferrara052003.asp> (March 20, 2006).

17. David Lawder, "US Jobless Claims Fall, More Job Growth Seen," Reuters, March 23, 2006 <http://today.reuters.com/business/ newsArticle.aspx?type=ousiv&storyID=2006-03-23T135440Z_01_ N23190558_RTRIDST_0_BUSINESSPRO-ECONOMY-DC.XML> (March 20, 2006).

18. Ibid.

19. Tom Raum, "Bush Tries to Strike a More Realistic Tone on Iraq, Spending His 'Political Capital'" Associated Press, March 21, 2006.

20. Matt Maurer and Albert Lang, "Early Look at Results of School Restructuring Under No Child Left Behind Shows Promise for Struggling Schools in Michigan," Center on Education Policy News Release, November 10, 2005.

21. Press Release, "Remarks by the President at Electronic Industries Alliance Government Industry Dinner," The Grand Hyatt Hotel, Washington, D.C., May 8, 2001, Office of the Press Secretary, the White House <http://www.whitehouse.gov/news/releases/2001/05/20010509. html> (March 20, 2006).

22. Press Release, "Remarks by the President at 'Ask President Bush' Event," Hara Complex, Dayton, Ohio, May 4, 2004, Office of the Press Secretary http://www.whitehouse.gov/news/releases/2004/05/20040504-5. html (March 20, 2006).

FURTHER READING

Burgan, Michael. *George W. Bush*. Minneapolis: Compass Point Books, 2004.

Gormley, Beatrice. *Laura Bush: America's First Lady*. New York: Aladin, 2003.

Hillstrom, Laurie Collier. *War in the Persian Gulf Primary Sources: From Operation Desert Storm to Operation Iraqi Freedom*. Detroit: UXL, 2004.

Sergis, Diana K., *Bush v. Gore: Controversial Presidential Election Case*. Berkeley Heights, NJ: Enslow Publishers, 2003.

Thompson, Bill and Dorcas. *George W. Bush*. Philadelphia: Mason Crest Publishers, 2003.

INTERNET ADDRESSES

"The White House: President George W. Bush"
<http://www.whitehouse.gov/>

"George Walker Bush"
<http://www.ipl.org/div/potus/gwbush.html>

"The War Behind Closed Doors"
<http://www.pbs.org/wgbh/pages/frontline/shows/iraq/>

INDEX

Page numbers for photographs are in **boldface** type.